A Walk In The Woods

An Incest Survivor's Guide
To Resolving The Past And Creating A Great Future

Nan O'Connor, MCC

For Dwight —
With much love and
deep appreciation
for your support on
this journey —
N

Published by Journey Publishing LLC
walkinthewoods.org

To Paul,
for holding my hand
every step of the way.
I love you.

A victim identity is the belief that the past is more powerful than the present, which is the opposite of the truth. It is the belief that other people and what they did to you are responsible for who you are now, for your emotional pain or your inability to be your true self. The truth is that the only power there is, is contained within this moment: It is the power of your presence. Once you know that, you also realize that you are responsible for your inner space now – nobody else is – and that the past cannot prevail against the power of the Now.

Eckhart Tolle
The Power of Now

TABLE OF CONTENTS

INTRODUCTION

At first I didn't know I was an incest survivor.
Then I knew and couldn't say it. Couldn't make the words come out of the place they were lodged in my throat.

Then my job was to say it. "Incest Survivor."

I used to call it the "I" word, and had to learn to say the words. Later my job was to own it. "I am an incest survivor." It was my job to say it a hundred thousand times. It was my job to tell the truth of my childhood. Speak it out loud.

Later still, it was my job to move beyond having my total identity be that of an incest survivor. I am a woman who is many things, and one of those things is an incest survivor. I embrace all of me, including the very strong part that was forged through surviving incest.

Today it is my job, part of my life purpose, to help others on their journey of healing from incest. How? By offering them a map and a compass for one of the most powerful experiences anyone can ever have. By helping them move through the fear, and by assuring them of the beauty they will encounter, and the amazing growth they will achieve.

Recently, a woman I was just getting to know shared with me an incident of when she was sexually abused as a child. She wanted to know if it was incest. She wanted to know if that one incident—thirty years later—could be contributing to difficulties that kept cropping up in her life. I shared a little of my experience and knowledge.

A few days later she asked me to go for a walk in the woods to talk. She needed to talk to someone who knew answers to some of her questions. She needed a witness to her truth, and a guide for moving forward. At the end of our walk, she said my words had changed her life. She's on her journey now and she knows I walk beside her.

As my husband and I discussed this experience, he said something that will not leave my head. He said, "You know, Nan, there are millions of people who really need a walk in the woods with you. Find a way to walk with them."

If you are in the process of healing from incest, or if you desire to start the process, this book is here to help you. It's not theory. It's not therapy. It's the experience of one who has made the journey. It will help you find your way, and most importantly, you will not walk alone.

ABOUT THIS BOOK

There are several ways to use this book.
You may choose to read it in a linear fashion, one chapter after another. In doing so, you will understand the flow of my healing and the way it unfolded for me.

That said, healing is not a linear process.

This book is written in manageable pieces, each based on one theme. While it generally follows the path of my healing, you can read whichever pieces speak to you at any given time. If anger is an issue for you today, then go to the chapters that deal with anger.

Getting "stuck" at some point in the healing process is common, with a feeling that progress is not happening. I remember times when I said I'd be happy to work on something if I just knew what it was. When you are stuck, flip through the pages until you find something that touches you. Chances are that's where you are stuck. Or you might see a topic that troubles you and you really want to avoid. This could be a clue that you could benefit by taking a little closer look.

I have been where you are now. As I received feedback on early drafts of this book, I learned that some readers felt intimidated by me. They had the impression that I really have my act together and am at a place they never could attain. I want to reassure you of something: I have been where you are. I have faced the darkness and feared the answers would never come. I have believed my life was such a wreck that it could never be salvaged. I have hit rock bottom, as they say. I know what it's like to claw my way through each day and wonder if it's even worth it. To believe that there is nothing—absolutely nothing—about me that had value or beauty. To know, in my heart of hearts, that I was unlovable.

I wrote this book from where I am today. But, I will never forget what it felt like to be where you are now. And this book is about the bridge between the two. It will take you by the hand and lead you over that bridge. Don't be intimidated. Be hopeful. You can do this!

Go at your own pace. It is very important to respect where you are in your healing process as you work through this book. At the end of each chapter, when you come to Your Actions, you might be ready to follow these suggestions—but you might not be ready as yet. Listen to yourself on this. You can always come back and try new actions when they feel right.

What I mean when I use the word "incest". Incest ordinarily is defined as sexual activity between two people who are considered, for moral and genetic reasons, too closely related to have such a relationship. I have no doubt that the need for healing is just as strong, however, as the result of sexual activity between any adult and any minor—whether blood-related or not—when there is a relationship of trust or a large power differential, enabling the adult to easily manipulate the minor. Such an adult might be a member of the clergy, a coach, a teacher or a trusted family friend. When I refer to incest, I am including this expanded scope.

An important distinction: I am an incest survivor sharing the journey of successfully piecing my life back together. But I am not a trained therapist. My story is not to be taken as therapeutic advice. I suggest all incest survivors work with trained professionals and support groups at critical points in their healing process. This book can be an important tool in that work, but it is not a substitute for professional help.

There is hope here! An artist friend of mine, from my incest survivors group, once made a cross for me with the word "hope" on it. For all these years, it has sat in a window where I see it many times a day. When she first gave it to me, I was in the deepest and darkest part of my journey, and "hope" sounded like a foreign word. This simple piece of art was a beacon for me when I felt lost. Someone out there believed there was a reason to hope!

Let this book be that beacon for you. I believe you can heal. Your present can become stronger than the past. There is nothing that has happened to you that you cannot move beyond. No matter how you feel at this moment, you do have it in you to take your own walk from devastation to wonderment.

Let's get started!

Part One: Resolving the Past

Chapter 1

FREEFALLING: A LEAP OF FAITH

We all know the definition of insanity—doing the same thing over and over again and expecting a different result. Sometimes, to change our lives, we have to drastically change our approach to our lives. I'm suggesting beginning your healing journey with a leap of faith.

MY STORY

My decision to heal didn't start out as a courageous one. It was a last resort.

I had tried all the external fixes. Addictive relationships hadn't worked. Neither had great business success at an early age. Nine years of therapy hadn't "fixed" me, nor had trying to buy happiness. Running away hadn't worked. Nothing had worked.

I took a leap of faith because I was miserable and had run out of options.

Here's how it started. One day one of my employees walked into my office and shut the door. Lately, she had seemed distracted and distant. Through tears, she told me how she had been raped by her father as a child and was just now dealing with it. She explained that it was really throwing her for a loop and asked me to be understanding and patient as she worked through this difficult period.

How I responded to her story startled me. I sank into a deep depression. When it continued after three weeks, I had to admit this wasn't about my compassion for my employee—this was about me. Something hidden deep inside had identified with what she was going through. She'd hit a nerve.

I'd been in and out of therapy for nine years. My therapist had once said that she suspected some sexual abuse in my past. I told her, truthfully, that I didn't remember anything happening. We never discussed it again.

After weeks of depression, however, I went back to the therapist, ready to look at my past. I gave her four weeks to fix me. Little did I know I was up against something that would rule out any quick fix.

When the first memory hit, I was making a left hand turn on to a busy street near my house. It was a flash, an image, a bolt of lightning. My life, thankfully, could never be the same.

The memories began the journey to reclaim my life. Instead of four weeks, this journey would last for years.

I could have chosen not to take the first step. Instead, I took a leap of faith. That was the beginning. I was freefalling with no idea where I would land. I simply took it on faith that I would be okay. And I was.

Here's what you must know before taking this leap: You will be okay. You really will. Surrender and fall into it, and the universe will support you. It will be scary as hell. It will take tremendous commitment. It will require strength you don't even know you have yet. And, it will be worth it.

If you choose to, you can do this! You absolutely can do this!

OUR WALK

When you talk about a "leap of faith," are you talking about some type of religious experience?

I think it's different for everyone. For me it wasn't about my belief in a deity who would take care of me. It was a trust—and, by the way, I wasn't big on trust at the time—that I could move into something without knowing where it would lead and be okay. At first, it was just a decision to trust even when I didn't really feel that I could.

How do you make a decision to trust something when you don't really feel trust?

Truthfully, I think it was a last resort. Nothing was working. What I had been doing wasn't going to get me where I needed to go. This had been proven over and over again. So, it was about saying that I was going to just surrender and fall and trust that where I landed couldn't be any worse than where I had already been. It was a conscious decision.

How do I start?

Start by letting go. Let go of trying to control everything. Admit that what you have done so far hasn't worked. Make a commitment to explore the unknown, believing it's not as scary as where you are right now.

Where did you land?

There's not just one freefall or one landing. You land in a place and stay there for a while to let things sink in and to rest. Then you freefall again. You arrive at a different place, explore it for a while and move on, as you are ready.

How long did you fall?

Here's the cool part. After you get used to it, you learn to use freefalling as a positive tool in of your everyday life! I freefall all the time now—on purpose. I've learned the power of letting go and not trying to control everything. Of letting things unfold naturally. Countless blessings have come to me that way. We'll talk more about that later.

Can you give an example of how you use freefalling in a positive way now, unrelated to your healing process?

Writing this book is a great example. My husband issued a challenge that scared the living daylights out of me. "You know Nan, there are millions of people who really need a walk in the woods with you. Find a way to walk with them." As I sat down with a blank page in front of me, I stepped into a brand new freefall, and this book is where I landed.

Is the freefall process just for people with repressed memories? Does it have relevance for someone who has been abused and has not repressed the abuse?

Absolutely. Whether you remember all of what happened or not, it still takes a leap of faith to step into that web of memories and emotions.

YOUR ACTION

Okay, are you ready to take your first action step? It's a simple one. Get a journal to write in. You are going to need it for a lot of the exercises in this book. You will come to use it, as I have, as an important tool for your healing.

In your journal, answer these questions:

- Is my life working now?
- What is the most radical change I would be willing to make if I knew it would bring healing?
- What's the worst that could happen if I decided to freefall into healing my life?

If you aren't ready for some of these questions yet, that's okay. Come back to them when you are.

Chapter 2

COMMITMENT

Freefalling is the first step in the healing process. It only works, however, if it's combined with commitment and action.

MY STORY

The decision to freefall was an impulse. Staying with the freefall meant making a commitment—a commitment to myself. I had never done that before.

From the outside, it looked like I was committed to myself. I was a successful businessperson who lived a "good" life. But I was surprised to realize that I had been committed to *appearing* to be okay—not really committed to doing the work necessary to be okay—not really committed to myself.

I had always been big on taking care of others. The weaker and more downtrodden they were, the more I was attracted to rescuing them. I felt a big commitment to those I was trying to save! Having built a very successful business, my job, I thought, was to safeguard the welfare of my 35 employees. I felt responsible for them.

It was a heavy load, and it kept me very busy, running and emotionally bankrupt. It also kept me from taking care of one particular person in the company—Nan O'Connor. I never looked inside of me. This approach had worked for me all my life—until now.

The commitment to heal required putting all that aside and deciding that I was going to put myself first. In our society, this is frowned upon. It's considered selfish. I'm here to tell you that it is the only way to give back to this world.

As I got into my healing process, I began to notice some subtle changes in some of those around me. By putting myself first in my life I angered some people. They were the very needy types who wanted me to be there for them at all times. My changing scared them. When I was focused on me, I wasn't as available to them. This didn't happen with everyone, of course. But it happened often enough that I noticed it.

I began to realize that dedication to my healing process would likely mean making a big shift in some of my relationships. Some people just can't deal with that. But I learned that was okay. It taught me a lot about people in my life. The

7

ones who were able to give me the space to do my healing work have continued to be some of my closest friends. The ones who couldn't went away. Painful? Yes. But looking back on it, it was perfect.

Seeing what was happening in my personal life, I also had to face the fear that being so occupied with healing would endanger my business. The energy and focus I needed to put into healing would mean that I had much less to give to the company.

But while I had a lot of fear about some of the consequences of starting my healing journey, I knew that if I didn't take care of myself—get my inner world right—I could never really be there for anyone else. And my life would never be what I hoped it could be.

So I fully committed to my healing and made it my mission. You know, there is a reason that organizations have mission statements. It helps them remember why they are doing what they do. It gives them a guiding light when things get foggy. As humans, we need guiding lights as well.

I wrote my healing mission statement down:

> *I am worth healing!*
> *Healing comes first!*
> *Nothing will stop me!*

This mission became my battle cry. I clung to it when everything else felt stripped away. It got me through. It guided my choices. It cost me at times—but only temporarily. And it never cost me anything that is of value to me today.

OUR WALK

So why did you have to make a choice between taking care of yourself and taking care of others? Couldn't you do both?

No. Not for a while. And not in the way I had been "taking care" of others. I had fallen into the trap of codependency. I took care of others so they would be there to take care of me. We all know that doesn't work. It's a fantasy. I had to become responsible for my own care. It was an inside job. Later, after I had done a lot of healing, I was able to be there for others again. At the beginning, though, it would have been like asking a person who is going down for the third time to save someone else. Couldn't be done.

When you say it cost you, what does that mean?

Many of the people who were in my life at the beginning of my healing process are not in it now. Some couldn't adjust as I shifted priorities.

I came to see some others as too unhealthy to be around. Prior to beginning the healing, I was drawn to abusive people. Their behavior was the way I had been raised as a child. They felt familiar to me. Now they had to go. They were simply too costly to have in my life.

My business suffered. The company I owned was a corporate communications company struggling against a declining economy and increased competition. There was one day that I knew that if I didn't re-focus from healing to my business, the company was likely to go under. I had spent years building the company. We had thirty-four employees counting on their paychecks. Every penny I had was in it. I made a hard decision. I chose myself.

There were times when healing felt like a full-time job. There were days I was simply too exhausted from the inner work I was doing to do anything else. One of the most important things in my life, the business, had to play second fiddle to healing. There were periods when I could focus on work, and it was enough to get by. But, even if it had meant losing the business, the price would have been worth it. Fortunately, my company survived along with me.

You also said that you never lost anything of real value. Didn't you value your friends and your business?

Sure. They played an important role in my life for a time. But what I have come to value today is very different from what I thought was important then. Now, I don't hold on to as much. I see people and businesses and experiences as teachers who come into our lives for a time to teach us what we need to learn. Many (not all) move on. That's okay. Plenty more are on the way!

Did you tell anyone about your Healing Mission Statement?

Yes. I found safe people with whom to share my mission, people who would support it. My husband. My therapist. The women in my incest survivors group. There is great power in saying your commitment out loud to witnesses.

A Healing Mission Statement sounds pretty silly to me. Sort of like all that positive thinking stuff that only lasts a little while. Why is it so important?

I'm usually pretty cynical myself about this kind of thing. The reason the mission statement is so powerful, I believe, is that incest survivors have had their power stripped away. Part of our healing is to get it back. Making a clear statement for ourselves is a way to start finding our power.

YOUR ACTION

The exercise here is to write your own Healing Mission Statement.

Here are some thought starters:

- What price have you paid for *not* putting yourself first?
- To whom do you look to take care of you?
- What would it be like if you found a way for all the stuff that keeps you stuck in unhappiness to go away? What would it be worth to make that happen?
- Are you willing to take a stand for yourself?
- What words can you say for yourself that are so compelling that even *you* will believe them?

Write your statement.
Make it visible. Put it where you will see it every day.
Say it out loud. Drive around in your car with the windows up and say it over and over again. Scream it!
Say it to others who are able to respect it.

Chapter 3

A SAFE PLACE

This healing work is scary. We need a safe space in which to do it. We need to be conscious about creating a safe place for ourselves. I'm talking about a safe physical space as well as a secure emotional context.

We need to focus on two things: making sure we are physically safe at all times and—equally critical—making sure the important relationships in our lives are safe ones. Many people think that a safe space is only about our physical environment. But, how can true safety exist if the people in our physical environment are unsafe people? We must look at both types of safety.

MY STORY

My childhood home was unsafe. On some level, that felt "normal" to me because I had never experienced anything else. Accordingly, choices made in creating my adult life had tilted toward an unsafe environment. I had selected several abusive friends and bosses and engaged in some unsafe behavior.

I would be drawn to a crazy or abusive friend, for example, to replay the turmoil and damage of my childhood. Or, I would experiment with drugs—something that was unsafe physically as well as legally.

At some point, in order to heal, I had to become intentional about creating a safe environment in which to do this work. This took time. It meant making big changes, but they were worth the effort. Having a strong foundation from which to move forward was crucial in the healing process.

There was a time in my life that I can clearly say the Hand of God touched me. It was when I chose to marry my husband. The psychologists will tell you that because I had grown up in an abusive home, the overwhelming odds were for me to marry an abusive man. Either a man who would abuse me or would abuse our children. It's pretty much a miracle that I chose to marry Paul O'Connor.

Paul grew up in a "normal" family. They had their garden-variety dysfunction, but nothing that would really mess someone up. Paul knows what it feels like to live in a family with happily married parents who are respectful to each other and their children. He knows about love that doesn't have inappropriate strings attached. He knows how to nurture and protect. Paul is simply the kindest man I have ever met. And I believe he saved my life.

The first step in creating a safe environment was to really let Paul in. Even though we had been married for some time, I had done a good job of distancing myself from him. Making the choice to enlist Paul as a supportive partner was essential in my healing process. Our marriage provided a safe harbor for this very difficult work.

It took more than a safe marriage, of course. While I hadn't picked an abusive husband, I had acquired a number of other relationships that were crazy and abusive. You know, the addictive relationships with people who are very unsafe.

These relationships were a constant source of turmoil and a big waste of energy. They ranged from abusive to codependent. They were all damaging. And I had created and owned a business in what I now consider to be a very abusive industry.

Over time, creating a safe world for myself meant ending a number of deep relationships that were unhealthy. It also meant selling my business. Not that all of this happened at once. These big, sweeping changes took place over a long time as I healed. First, I had to get safe on a very basic level.

There were two books that were an enormous support to my healing: *The Courage to Heal* and *The Courage to Heal Workbook.* There's a really great section in the workbook that guided me through creating a safe space in my life, and I highly recommend it. I did things like create a list of reliable people to call when the process became too intense and I felt as if I was losing ground. I kept their phone numbers with me at all times.

To feel physically protected, I made a safe space in my house where I could always go and feel secure. I took a self-defense course. I got a Rottweiler to accompany me on my runs. I collected stuffed animals to surround myself with and hug.

Some of these measures may sound extreme. But I did whatever it took for me to feel safe. Some measures were objective responses to dangers that were actually present. Others helped calm the residual fear of harm that I felt because of the abuse. Some of these actions were permanent—I still use them today to ensure my safety. Others were useful at the time, and today I find I no longer need them.

Emotional safety was, and is, important, too. I created a set of boundaries. Those boundaries defined what kind of behavior I would allow in my life and what I wouldn't. (See the Table of Contents for more on boundaries.) And I joined an incest survivors group where it would be safe to tell my story and feel my feelings.

OUR WALK

If I have never experienced a safe environment, how can I even begin to create one for myself?

Use outside help until you develop your own internal mechanism for knowing what is safe and what isn't. You may want to work with a personal coach or therapist to help you at first. Over time, you will begin to know for yourself what's safe and what's not.

Here's an important point: It's not that you don't *have* the internal mechanism to know what's safe—rather, you had to ignore it for so long to live in your unsafe home that tuning into it now is difficult. Over time, as you experience safety, your internal "gut" feelings will become stronger. *Always* listen to your gut. It's almost never wrong.

Are you saying that I have to get rid of all the unsafe people in my life before I can begin to heal?

No, I'm not saying that. This is not a linear process. You create some safety, you heal some, you create some more safety, you heal some more. It comes in fits and starts. What I do know is that as you heal, you will tolerate less and less from your environment that isn't safe.

I don't understand what you mean about boundaries. Tell me more.

This is one of the most powerful concepts I have ever found. Boundaries are a set of guidelines that you create for yourself and then communicate, as needed, to others. I started using boundaries instinctively during my healing process and then learned formally about them at Coach U when I was learning to become a professional coach. My written list of boundaries includes things like:

- No one may raise his/her voice in anger when speaking to me.
- I don't maintain relationships with disrespectful people.
- I don't allow drunks in my life.

My boundaries help me teach others how to treat me. At this point my boundaries have become so strong that I usually don't have to communicate them verbally. People can just tell that I am someone to treat respectfully. Years ago, this wasn't the case. I had to set very strong verbal boundaries. I remember telling a friend, "The way you spoke to me is abusive. I will not allow you to abuse me." Eventually this person couldn't be in my life anymore because she couldn't respect this boundary.

(I give a lot more information about boundaries later in the book.)

YOUR ACTION

Take the action necessary to make your life a Danger Free Zone. Begin by filling out this Safety Criteria Check List. Read each item and put a checkmark next to the statement only if it is true for you.

Check if true	**Safety Criteria Check List**
	I am not living with physical abuse.
	I am not living with emotional abuse.
	I do not fear for my physical safety.
	I have a list of support people I can call if I feel panicked.
	I am in a support group of incest survivors.
	My list of support people is written out (with their phone numbers) and stored in a place I can easily find it.
	I have a therapist I trust and see regularly.
	I have a place of safety, outside my home, where I can go if violence occurs in my home.
	I don't have sex when I don't want to.
	I have a private place to keep my personal writings.
	I have a place in my home that feels safe to me where I can go and be undisturbed.

	I have set boundaries as to when and where I will work on my abuse issues—so this process remains healthy for me.
	I have at least one person with whom I can safely share what I am going through.
	I do not engage in activities that endanger my life or my health.
	I live in a secure home.
	My work environment is physically safe.
	My work environment is emotionally safe.

Now that you have taken a safety inventory, let's look at the conditions you would like to change, and when. Keep in mind that probably you will not be able to change everything at once.

There are some things that you may feel compelled to change immediately, because they are simply not acceptable to you as they are. Others may take a little working up to. Yet others may need to wait a longer time until you are ready.

Look at the following chart. For the items you wish to change, place a checkmark in the column that describes the timeframe that feels right to you. I want to encourage you to make as many changes as you can to feel safe without pushing yourself to the point that it is harmful.

Safety Criteria Check List	Change Now	Change Within One Month	Change Within 3-6 Months	Change Within One Year	Change In The Future
I am not living with physical abuse.					
I am not living with emotional abuse.					
I do not fear for my physical safety.					
I have a list of support people I can call if I feel panicked.					

I am in a support group of incest survivors.					
My list of support people is written out (with their phone numbers) and stored in a place where I can easily find it.					
I have a therapist I trust and see regularly.					
I have a place of safety, outside my home, where I can go if violence occurs in my home.					
I don't have sex when I don't want to.					
I have a private place to keep my personal writings.					
I have a place in my home that feels safe to me where I can go and be undisturbed.					
I have set boundaries as to when and where I will work on my abuse issues —so this process remains healthy for me.					
I have at least one person with whom I can safely share what I am going through.					
I do not engage in activities that endanger my life or my health.					
I live in a secure home.					
My work environment is physically safe.					
My work environment is					

emotionally safe.					

Now, make an action plan for changing the items you would like to change. Here's an example:

Action	By When	Status
Write a list of support people and their phone numbers and keep it in my safe place.	10/15	
Buy a lockbox for my personal writings.	10/29	
Join a support group	11/15	
Get a new job	12/31	

Chapter 4

A SUPPORT STRUCTURE

MY STORY

"Join an incest survivors group." Those words from Karen, my therapist, felt as if someone had plugged me into an electrical socket. Shocking! An incest survivors group? You have got to be kidding! Me, in a group? No way!

Karen explained why. "What I have to offer you isn't enough. You need to be with people going through the same thing you are, guided by therapists trained to help incest survivors."

I still balked, certain that I'd be better off working on it alone. Same way I've done everything else in my life.

She didn't relent. "Join a group, Nan. I can't help you if you don't. Here are some numbers to call."

Best move I've ever made in my life.

Other incest survivors are the only people who can truly understand what you are going through. While others may *try* to understand, incest survivors *understand*. They really understand. They understand on a level I thought impossible.

I spent five years in that group, every Wednesday night. It's the wisest time I have ever invested in myself.

Those people were amazing. We, collectively, were amazing. Let me tell you, there is powerful, powerful energy in such a group.

When the memories came and overwhelmed me, and I felt like a small child standing in the ocean being knocked over by waves and there wasn't enough time to get back on my feet, I would have drowned without that safe retreat and those helping hands.

OUR WALK

What if I'm not one for groups? Isn't working with a therapist enough?

No. Absolutely not. We need a safe group of people who are fellow travelers on this journey. We need a group of peers to validate our experience. Some will be farther along than you—they will help lead the way. Others will lag behind—they will show you how far you have come and allow you to give back.

Is it better for those in the group to be people you know, or people you don't know?

I loved the fact that the people in my group were not in my daily life. (A couple became life-long friends, by the way. But for years we only met in the group.) It allowed me to open myself up in a way that I couldn't have otherwise. They gave me a place where I could act in ways I never would have with people who knew me.

One vivid memory I have is walking up to a stage in front of hundreds of business and media people to receive an award as a finalist for Entrepreneur of the Year. That audience could not have imagined that, just an hour before, I had been in my group, sitting on the floor, screaming at a large brown bear! I found it very ironic. The business community thought they knew me, but the people who *really* knew me were in my incest survivors group. What absolute freedom there was in being with them!

How do I find an incest survivors group? How do I know which group is right for me?

Ask people you trust. If you have a therapist, ask him/her to give you several names. Get referrals from crisis hotlines or the local Council on Child Abuse.

When you've collected names, call the group leader to get a "gut" feel for the ones that feel right to you. I remember calling four or five group leaders, and no one really struck the right chord for me. Then I picked up a voice mail from my therapist giving me one more name. I called her, Linda, and I *knew* I had found the right one. Don't settle. Interview until you find a place you feel comfortable.

Questions To Ask When You Interview For A Group

Is this group restricted only to incest survivors?

I believe you need a group for incest survivors, period. A general therapy group is not targeted enough for what you will need.

What are the rules for the group?
There will be rules such as these:
- *Attend regularly*
- *Treat others with respect*
- *Maintain a safe physical environment*
- *Come to sessions drug and alcohol free*

How often does it meet?
I recommend a group that meets weekly.

What are your (the leader's) credentials?
Verify that the leader is a professional therapist with experience leading incest survivor groups.

Is this an ongoing group or is it a new group? If it's ongoing, how long has it been in existence? Do you have an end date for the group?
I prefer open-ended groups rather than one with an end date. I was in my group for five years. At the start, I had no idea I would need it that long, but I did. And I was so glad that it would be around as long as I needed it.

How many are in the group?
I would not want to be in a group with more than eight people.

What is the duration of each session?
One and one half hours to two hours is a good length for a group of six to eight.

YOUR ACTION

Put the following on your "to do" list and do them within the next 10 days:

- Get the names of at least four people who are leading incest survivor groups.
- Interview them.

- Select a group.
- Join!

Once you have joined, remember to:
- Participate
- Keep going even when you don't want to – it's worth it!
- Remember that it's the times you don't feel like going to the group that you may most need to be there.

Chapter 5

THE HEALING PROCESS

As humans we strive to create order out of chaos. That's why we develop processes, to give us a map and compass to find our way. To share with others what we have learned through trial and error so they can benefit from our experiences. For something as multifaceted as healing from incest, a process can be invaluable.

MY STORY

One of the biggest events in my life was when a friend of mine gave me a book called *The Courage to Heal.* I was about three months into incest recovery when this incredible book came into my life. I lived with that book at my side for about five years. What impressed me most was this—for the first time, I saw parts of a process spelled out. That made all the difference in the world for me.

A process. I understood processes. In business, I had a system for everything. You give me a process, and I can move mountains! It was like I had been wandering in the dark wilderness and suddenly someone turned on a light.

The process was not totally defined—it had missing pieces. So, over time, I pieced together a lot of different things to create the system that worked best for me. But knowing that healing could be approached from a process standpoint gave me a handle on moving forward.

OUR WALK

So it sounds like The Courage to Heal *gave you a start on finding a process. Was that all there was to it? Read one book and heal yourself?*

No, of course not. *The Courage to Heal* was a great start because it gave me a lot of encouragement that there was a way to "process" the incest issues I was dealing with. And, I learned from it that there were different aspects to the healing process. The book broke the process down into more manageable pieces.

Then how did you find the process you ended up using?

I pieced together a lot of different things. Things I learned in books, from an incest survivor group, from therapy. Probably the most important discovery, however, were the tools I was learning in my studies to become a professional coach. Up to that point my understanding had deepened, but I didn't know what *actions* to take to use that understanding to change my life on a sustained basis. The coaching tools gave me instruments for action.

What is this coaching? And what are the tools coaching uses?

Coaching is a profession that helps people get where they are trying to go easier and faster. I am a certified by the International Coach Federation as an MCC (Master Certified Coach). I have had a coaching practice since 1998 and I specialize in coaching small business owners.

A lot of the tools that coaching uses are found in this book. These include setting boundaries and standards for yourself. Taking very good care of yourself. Understanding how your needs drive your decision-making. Learning to orient your life around your values. Getting rid of objectionable things and/or relationships that you are tolerating in your life.

So are you going to outline a step-by-step process to heal?

This book is written to share with you the steps I took to heal. You can pick and choose the parts that will be most beneficial to you.

Does the process go in a certain order?

Although the process is not linear, there is a basic progression. That's how this book is organized; however, you will probably find yourself jumping around, depending on where you are in your recovery on any given day.

You were a business owner with time and money. What about those who don't have those resources?

It's even harder when time and money are scarce. To tell the truth, my company went into debt during my healing process—so time and money *were* a factor for me as well. But, it is true that I managed to carve out enough of both to focus on my healing. I know that others may find it hard to do that.

If you lack money, you will have to look harder to find support—but you can find it. Therapy can be expensive. Check out employee assistance programs. Many Councils on Child Abuse offer free or low-cost survivor groups. Most therapists will work with you on a fee-structure based on your ability to pay.

As for time, you'll have to get creative. I know a single mom of three who pools resources with two other moms. During the week, each one has a night that she cooks for all three families. That means each mom gets two nights off a week. Think of the things you could do to create some time in your busy life.

YOUR ACTION

- At first, all I ask you to do is trust that there is a process to heal and that you will find it.

- Use this book, and other books on incest (like *The Courage To Heal*), to find the process that works best for you. Here are some things to remember:
    o Having someone tell you what worked for him or her can be very powerful. Try it on for yourself and see if it works for you. It may or it may not. This isn't an exact science.
    o What you need today may not be what you need tomorrow. Become aware of all the things you can do to promote your healing and use them when you are ready for them.
    o Do things, as you are ready to do them. You might read in this book about something that I am suggesting you do, but you might not be ready for it. Trust yourself on this. Come back to it later. There are things that fell on deaf ears with me for years, but the time came when those actions suddenly fit perfectly.

- Use your incest survivors group to share healing techniques. Again, you will be the best judge of what's right for you and when to use it.

Chapter 6

TRUSTING THE HEALING PROCESS

It's the fear that stops us from healing. As children we couldn't handle what was happening, so we stuffed it down deep inside. Then our life didn't work very well anymore. It couldn't work because we had unresolved feelings and experiences that stunted our growth.

That's the fear at work. Fear ... that we will uncover those hidden feelings and they will drive us mad. Fear ... that we won't be able to handle the truth. So we keep ourselves as far from the truth as possible. Until *that* drives us mad.

Then the leap of faith happens. The process starts to unfold, and we move into uncharted territory. We ride the waves of recovery and hang on for dear life.

Take all of this on faith until you have experienced it long enough to feel it's true. *You can trust the healing process.*

MY STORY

My incest recovery was filled with starts and stops. I would make great progress, then hit a brick wall. I called it being "stuck"—numerous periods of being immobilized and not knowing how to get the healing process moving again. It was horrible. Days, weeks, months ... no progress. What was next? Why couldn't I find the key? Then suddenly a rush of memories, a flood of feelings, would knock me off my feet. It was a full-time job just dealing with all that was surfacing.

Over the years, I came to understand that this ebb and flow *is* the healing process and it exists whether you have always remembered your abuse or are recovering memories for the first time. And, there is an innate wisdom to this starting and stopping. For a while there is nothingness, then a flood. Things come as we are ready to deal with them. That's when they pour out. They keep coming as long as we can handle them. Then, a pause. We may feel "stuck," but we are actually resting. Healing. Taking time to breathe.

I have gained tremendous respect for the ability of survivors to heal, and for the healing process *itself.* There is an inherent intelligence in the process. I don't know where it comes from, but I am so thankful it is there. This innate wisdom has never let me down. It regulates the pace of my healing in a way that keeps me safe. When I have become too overwhelmed, the process has backed off and let me relax. When I have been ready to move forward, it has given me the opening to do so. It will do the same for you. I have no doubt.

Fairly early on I came to trust this process. Given that I wasn't prone to trust much of anything back then, that's an amazing thing. What started as a leap of faith became a profound confidence. Even when I was really, really scared, I knew I could count on the wisdom of the process and an eventual beneficial result for me.

And here's the real gift: over time, this trust in the process evolved into a trust in myself, and eventually a trust in life itself. Now that's a beautiful thing!

OUR WALK

I'm still not sure what you mean by trusting the healing process. Can you be more specific?

Yes. Bottom-line, I mean that you will never have to deal with *anything* you are not ready to deal with. Nothing will come up that you can't handle, even if it takes some help from others. This "wisdom" knows what you are ready for—and what must wait until later.

Does being stuck mean that you are not having any new memories, or that you have reached some kind of halt with the memories you are dealing with?

Being stuck may or not be related to how the memories are flowing. You may be stuck when you sense there is a memory lurking, but it won't surface. Or, it may have nothing to do with memories. It may simply be when you don't know the next step to take to advance your healing.

You say there is a wisdom to the process. How do you tap into this wisdom?

Become still enough to hear it. It's not "hearing" like a voice, but more like a *knowing*. Some would call it intuition or instinct.

Give me specific ways to become still, so I can hear the wisdom of the healing process.

28

I'm sure it's different for everyone. And, for me, different ways worked at different times. Here are some techniques I used:

- *Meditation.* I used this when I was calm enough to sit down and meditate. I centered my mind on my breathing. In. Out. In. Out. Let everything be. No judgment. No trying to make things different. Just being. It helped me get in touch with the "knowing."

- *Journaling.* Writing in my journal was a very good way to get in touch with my inner wisdom. It was particularly helpful when I was too anxious to sit and meditate. I would just start writing, whatever came up. I didn't care how the writing came out—it was only for me, not for other eyes. It is amazing how writing can tap into the heart of things and provide guidance.

- *Prayer.* When things became overwhelming and I didn't know where to turn, I would pray. I'm not religious in a traditional sense. Sometimes my prayers would begin with "I don't know if you are there or not, but if you are ..." It always worked. Brought me peace. And, in time, answers.

- *Inner Child Work.* I went to a seminar given by John Bradshaw where I learned how to connect with my Inner Child. Inner Child work was a terrific way to tap into the wisdom of the healing process. (See more about Inner Child work later in this book.)

- *Exercise.* I used running as a way to take the keyed-up physical feelings away so I could hear inside myself. This is a way I tapped into the process.

YOUR ACTION

Take baby steps toward trusting your healing process. For example, try browsing through this book and looking at the "Your Action" segments of the chapters. Find something that hits a chord with you. Make sure the action feels "right" (that means it's something that feels safe, that you are ready to do, and that will possibly stretch you a bit). Give it a try.

Use this first baby step as a way to begin to trust your process. I believe you will find that you *know* what you need when you need it.

If some of what I'm recommending feels too wide open, then work with your therapist or within your incest survivor group to know where you are in your process and how to keep facing forward.

Over time, you will start to trust your "gut." You will become expert at tuning into what you need and when. Above all, you will understand that the healing process will never give you more to handle than you are capable of at that time.

Chapter 7

WHEN THE PRESENT TRIGGERS THE PAST

For an incest survivor, there are times when our emotions don't match up with the current situation of our life. Our emotions overpower our logic. When this experience comes, it's likely that some event in the present has triggered emotions from events of the past. At such times, our reaction may cause others to look at us as if we've grown three heads.

MY STORY

I was playing racquetball with a friend when, for no discernable reason, I became paralyzed with fear. It was as if someone had kicked me in the stomach and I could barely move. Why? I had no idea. A routine Saturday morning, playing a game I loved—and suddenly I was scared to death. *What was going on?*

Having lunch with a man, discussing business, suddenly I felt like a small child. I was afraid of him. I couldn't stand him. But I hardly even knew him. He had done absolutely nothing wrong, yet I had the strongest urge to get up from the table and run away. *What was going on?*

One October morning I went out to go for a run. Summer had turned to fall, the air was crisp—a beautiful day. But I was overwhelmed with fear and sadness. I turned around and went back inside. I spent the rest of the day under the covers. *What was going on?*

In each of these episodes, something innocent or neutral triggered feelings from dangerous and painful events in my past. I'm sure that similar "echoes" come to everyone at times. But for incest survivors, these feelings can be overwhelming. And unless you understand what is happening, the situation can be disconcerting to the point of near paralysis.

At first, as these things happened, I panicked because I thought I must be going crazy. If the feelings hadn't been so strong, I would have tried to deny them, but they were too overwhelming. All I could do was try to survive them. For me, this meant relying on the support structure I had built—calling my therapist or someone from my incest survivors group. Or talking to my husband.

31

Over time, I became more practiced at processing these episodes. I learned that they could be useful in my healing. It became clear that the feelings being triggered were unresolved issues surfacing from my childhood. These issues were coming to the fore now because I was finally ready to deal with them.

And deal with them I did. Nothing would come up that I *wasn't* able to deal with safely at that time. Ever. I learned to trust that.

These triggering moments became a part of healing. Whenever I would begin to feel emotions not appropriate to the current situation, I would tell myself that whatever I was feeling was *not* happening now, that it was *old*. If I was so distressed that I couldn't communicate effectively with myself, then I got someone else to tell me.

Ultimately, when I felt safe enough, I let the emotions lead me to whatever long-ago events they were related. And I *felt* the feelings about what had happened. I asked others to validate those feelings. I learned to validate them myself.

This is how you heal. You are feeling today, here and now, what you could not feel as it was happening. And, for the first time in your life, you can validate those feelings. You can know that you weren't crazy as a child. You can wrap yourself in love and protection—the love and protection you should have had then, but didn't.

Healing is about going back to all the unclaimed feelings and embracing them. In this way, you give to yourself all the things you should have been given as a child. Respect, safety, protection, honor. The process requires that either you give these qualities to yourself, or you get them from your support system until you are able to do it on your own.

It is the wonder of my life that I could really do this and that it really worked. There *was* a way out of the confusion and pain I had felt all my life. Even now, it's so beautiful it brings tears to my eyes.

OUR WALK

How did you cope when strong emotions were triggered?

I learned to separate what I was feeling from what was really going on today. That would help me get to a safe place inside. I learned to understand that the feelings were *old* and not related to my reality today.

If I couldn't do this myself, I would ask for help from others whom I trusted. I would get very specific about what I was feeling. Then I would get very specific about what was really going on today. For example, when I felt panic and fear, I would do a reality check. Was anyone really trying to hurt me today? Was anyone raping me right now? No, it just *felt* that way. Okay, I know that I am safe today.

Then, once I knew that it was not happening *now*, I would get support to feel the feelings. I would do this in group, or with my therapist, or with my husband. Or, when I felt able, on my own.

What about anger? Where does it fit in with all this?

Anger was certainly one of the feelings that eventually came up. For me, the fear and pain came first, then the anger. When it came—and, believe me, it was big—I handled it like I did all the other feelings. I looked at what was really happening and asked if my anger was appropriate to the situation today or if it might be about the past. When I realized it was about the past, I let myself feel it. I did whatever I could (that didn't damage myself or others) to let it out.

This doesn't sound very appealing to me, this stuff about having to feel all your feelings. I don't like feeling things that hurt me. Isn't that damaging to me?

It is hard to move toward our strong feelings. We'd rather run from them. I've mentioned that the healing process takes commitment. This is where the commitment to yourself comes in—to feel something you have avoided feeling your whole life.

The truth is, the effect is the opposite of damaging. It's healing. The feelings are there, stuck deep inside. Until you get them out, they haunt you. They infect you with depression. Or, you may feel them erupt in inappropriate and damaging ways in situations that don't call for that level of intensity.

The way I came to be able to feel my feelings was to learn that they are *just* feelings. That's *all* they are. They don't hurt you when you let them move through and out. Suppressing them gives them negative power over you. Releasing them frees you.

YOUR ACTION

When you find yourself having stronger emotions than the current situation calls for, stop and take inventory. If you are really freaking out and need support beyond yourself, then get to your support structure ASAP. It may be your therapist, incest survivor group, a trusted friend or partner. The first order of business is to get to a safe place.

Once you feel safe, walk yourself through the following (or do this with someone who can support you):

- Are these feelings related to just the current situation or are they "bigger" than the situation really calls for?
- When, as a child, did I feel these kinds of feelings?
- Honor whatever comes up.
- Is that same thing happening right now? How is today different from the past when I had the same feelings?
- Become very clear on the reality of today. On what's *really* happening today.
- Make a list of the resources you have today that you did not have as a small child.
- Do your best to separate today from the past. Get present to what is really happening today.
- Then your work splits into two tracks.
  - The first track is to handle today. What action do you need to take to resolve the situation that is actually happening today?
  - The second track is to address the past issues that created feelings that today's situation triggered. Usually something was left undone. Either feelings were suppressed or action was not taken that should have been taken. Or you needed something you did not get.

Here's an example: When I was having lunch with the man I didn't know well and we were discussing business, my feelings about my stepfather were triggered. There was something about this guy that set off my internal alarms.

As I sorted out in my head the questions I have just laid out above, I realized that this guy wasn't my stepfather. I had never met him before. The reality of today was that he had never hurt me. So, I was able to deal with him in a business-like manner. (I will also tell you, however, that because he sparked such strong negative feelings, I trusted my "gut" that he was someone I never wanted to be close to.)

Then, I did quite a bit of work concerning my stepfather. That was not a quick fix. It took a lot of different work over the years. Things like going through exercises in which the strong adult that I am today protected the vulnerable child

I was then. Also, actions like writing him a letter telling him how I really feel about him. Doing physical things to let the anger out. Beating him up with a baseball bat (a pillow substituted for the real person, of course).

Over time, as you take these steps, you will become really good at noticing, in the moment, when the present is triggering things from the past. I have gotten to where I usually notice it as it is happening, make a mental note to deal with it later, and continue in the present without the past influencing it. Then, after the fact, I go and do my work with the past. The more you do, the easier and faster it gets. Eventually, it's no big deal. It's more like "Oh yeah, this is what's happening. Okay."

As noted in the quote from Eckart Tolle that opened this book, there is *always* more power in our present than in our past. For an incest survivor, this conviction is fundamental to healing.

Chapter 8

OVERWHELM

When we start dealing with our past—I mean *really* dealing with it—there are times we go into overwhelm mode. By that, I mean that the feelings that come up can knock us off our feet temporarily. Pay attention to the word "temporarily" because it's very important. Overwhelm mode is not a fixed state that will last forever—it only feels that way at the time it happens.

I've already said that my experience causes me to trust the healing process—to believe we will never be given more to handle than we are able. And that's true. Still, there are times that feel very overwhelming, and it's important to know how to deal with them.

MY STORY

When I read a chapter in *The Courage to Heal* called The Emergency Stage, I knew for the first time what was going on. I was early in my healing process and I felt totally overwhelmed. Some days I couldn't get out of bed. The feelings of fear kept washing over me and I was paralyzed.

It was so validating to know there was something called The Emergency Stage. Others had been there and come out with their skin on. And, it was temporary.

Throughout my healing, The Emergency Stage came and went. It was most intense at first. Just getting through the day was a full-time job. This lasted several months. Later, it came and stayed for shorter periods of time. And, because I had been there before, I wasn't as startled by it.

A friend gave me a great analogy that I used often. She said the healing process is like standing in the ocean during a terrible storm. At first, the waves are constant. They knock you off your feet again and again. You usually don't make it back to your feet before you are knocked down once more. Gradually, the big waves come a little less often. You have a bit of time in between to get back up and pull yourself together. Eventually, they are smaller and farther apart. You let them pass by you without knocking you down. And finally, you simply are able to enjoy a day at the beach.

OUR WALK

What causes The Emergency Stage?

I'm sure therapists would have a technical answer for this. From the perspective of someone who has lived through it, I would say that we spend a lifetime *not* dealing with the incest. We build a world that avoids the memories, feelings, and integration of that violation. When we begin to heal, we open the floodgates. We are now facing what we have feared most, dealing with what really happened and how that has impacted us. There's a lot of stuff that starts bubbling up. It can feel overwhelming.

The analogy is great, but I would like to know specific things you did to get through the overwhelming periods.

I took extremely good care of myself and I honored where I was. Here are some specifics:
- I allowed myself to be scared and immobilized.
- I told my business partners that I was going through a really tough time emotionally and that I would be focusing more on getting through it than on the business.
- I surrounded myself with my safety support structure.
- I had a list of friends I could call and talk to when things got to be too much.
- I did a lot of work in my survivors group.
- I ate comfort food.
- I wrote in my journal.
- I got massages when doing so felt comforting.
- I used exercise to feel strong when this felt called for.

YOUR ACTION

Create a plan for what you will do to take care of yourself when you feel overwhelmed. Do it at a time that you *don't* feel overwhelmed. Write it down. Step by step. Keep it handy. Then, when you go into overwhelm, you don't have to figure out what to do. You only have one thing to remember: Go to your overwhelm plan and act on it.

It might look something like this:

1. Put both feet on the floor and take 10 deep breaths.
2. Go to my safe place.
3. Call Mary. Her number is _____.
4. If Mary is not there, call _____. Her number is _____.
5. Tell her that I need her to tell me that this will all be okay. That I am safe today. That what happened in the past is not happening now.

Write your step-by-step plan now. Make several copies and keep them in handy places.

Chapter 9

MEMORIES

A friend of mine was in a head-on collision. Immediately after impact, despite being seriously injured, he crawled out of the rubble to check on the people in the other car. The police report recounts bystanders seeing him walking around helping others for at least 30 minutes. He never lost consciousness. For years, however, if you asked him about the accident, he couldn't tell you anything. Didn't remember a thing between the point of impact and several hours later.

Years later the memories of the accident slowly returned.

We've all heard these kinds of stories. They are commonplace. We never question whether the accident really happened.

Child sexual abuse is like a head-on collision. The trauma is often beyond our ability to process at the time. We forget it as it happens. Only later, when it is safe, are we able to recover our memories of what really occurred.

MY STORY

The first flash of memory came out of the blue. It was a frame—just one single frame—of an entire scene that I could not remember. Then nothing. Just fog. Literally fog. When I tried to remember what had happened—that the one flash of memory had come out of—all I saw was black and gray fog.

The safer I made my life, the more pieces of memory surfaced. First, through the fog, all I saw was the corner of the roof of a building. I was looking up at it as if I were way down on the ground. I knew it wasn't a house. It was some kind of out-building, I thought. Maybe a garage or a boathouse.

Over many, many months, pieces of the memory fell into place. When I was ten, my mother left me overnight with a 45-year-old man who worked for our family business. He had gotten drunk and started chasing me through the house. He shoved a dishtowel in my mouth, held a butcher knife up to my face and raped me. It happened out by a pool. That's what the corner of the building was. The pool house. It was the first day of fall—you know, when the angle of the light changes and the air is crisp for the first time that season.

That memory explained so much. Like why I swam in my clothes for two years starting when I was ten. Or why I felt a huge depression every fall when the

41

weather changed. Or why for no apparent reason I suddenly was very, very angry with the man who worked for my family.

That memory was the first of many. Four different men abused me over a period of many years. There are lots of things I forgot in order to survive. I'm sure there are things I *still* don't remember. Every now and then a new memory comes to me.

Memories used to scare me. Now they don't, because I have learned something very important. I never remembered anything I couldn't handle, even if it required help from others to deal with it. If we remember it, it's because we are ready to use it to heal. I know this is true. You can trust it. You can trust this absolutely.

OUR WALK

This memory stuff sounds really traumatic. How did you make it through?

Processing memories—making them part of our truth—gets easier the more you do it. My first memory took over a year to process. Now I usually process a memory in a couple of days. Sometimes a couple of hours.

Are the memories you have now as intense as when the memories began?

The intensity of these newer memories may or may not be as strong as the earlier memories—but the processing time is much shorter, because I know the drill. And, I have had time to put memories in perspective. I have come to understand that they are just memories. They can't harm me today. I also know that they are coming up to be beneficial to me, so I don't resist them as I once did.

When you talk about "processing" memories, what exactly does this mean?

This is probably different for everyone. For me, it meant a certain set of steps I went through when a memory emerged:

- First, I made my world very safe. I surrounded myself with the things and people who felt safe to me. I kept my dogs at my side. I kept my world simple. I didn't take risks while I was doing memory work.
- I spent a lot of time in my safe place—for me that was in my bedroom.

- As memories came, I wrote them in my journal.
- When it felt okay to do so, I read them to my husband or talked to my therapist about them.
- Finally, again as it felt safe, I shared them with the women in my incest survivors group.
- Last, I never told them to anyone who might question the truth of my memories or dishonor them in any way. Never.

Do I have to remember everything that happened to me in order to heal?

I don't believe we have to remember *everything* to heal. We just need to remember what we need to remember in order to heal—that doesn't necessarily mean everything that happened to us. It means the things that keep us stuck.

How do I make my memories surface? I'm ready to get this over with!

You can't rush it. Memories come when you are ready to deal with them and not before. In fact, trying to force the matter may slow things down. There are some steps you can take to help the memories emerge once they start, however. Journaling was very helpful to me. Meditation—letting go—also helped. I did a lot of bodywork, like massage. I've found that my memories are often stuck in my body and a healing massage can help to release them. So does physical exercise. I trained for and ran half marathons while I was doing my most intense memory work.

The key is to live your life in a way in which you feel safe. Memories come up when you are safe enough to handle them. And remember, you will not remember anything you are not capable of handling. Ever.

I don't get it. I have always remembered everything. Every single detail. I can't imagine not remembering. Is this book just for people who forgot their abuse?

This book is for everyone who was abused. Period. Whether you forgot or remembered, the damage is the same. This book is about healing that damage. I write about recovering memories, because that was an important part of my healing and is such a huge issue for many survivors.

I have always remembered my abuse. Does that mean it wasn't traumatic?

Absolutely not! Some people retain their memories and some lose them. If you have remembered your abuse all along, then you are on your way to healing. You already know what you are dealing with and can take steps to heal from it.

YOUR ACTION

This action is about creating an environment that makes it safe for memories to come up. Refer to the chapter on A Safe Place and review the checklist. See if there are things you would like to change about your environment.

Chapter 10

BELIEVING

Whether we are recovering memories or have retained them all along, it's almost always hard to believe these things really happened. For years, I struggled with believing. Every now and then, a thought popped into my mind: "What if I made all this up?" But why would I ever make this up? I wouldn't. It would serve no purpose. This work is much too hard to inflict on myself without cause. No one would go through this who didn't have to.

And then I remember the car accident involving my friend. No one questions that the accident happened just because he couldn't remember it for years. How dare anyone question that my incest memories are not just as valid! Not anyone—not even *me*!

MY STORY

Coming to believe was a moment to moment, back and forth kind of thing for me. The memories came, and I flowed between believing them and telling myself I must have made them up. My head and my heart were at war.

My heart said that Daddy would never do this to me, that others who loved me couldn't have done such things, that my mother would have figured it out and protected me.

However my head said that, when the memories came, they explained so much I had never understood about my life. They filled in the blank spaces. Like missing pieces of a puzzle, they helped my life make sense.

Also, my head said that no one planted these ideas in my brain. No one was pressing me to remember things. An employee going through incest recovery had triggered my memories. They came on their own without any encouragement from me or anyone else.

And I knew that making this up made no sense. I got nothing out of it. It was too painful—much too painful.

For me, it was like the process of believing that someone who has died suddenly is really dead. At times, the realization is in your face. Too much in your face. So, for protection, part of you starts to believe it's not true. Even though you know it is. You pray to wake up from the nightmare of this knowledge. But you can't. Every time you wake up, there it is. Over time you make peace with it.

It took me years to make peace with the reality of having been sexually abused. And, even now, I'd rather not believe it. But I know that a significant part of my healing is to honor the truth of my own life.

OUR WALK

Why do you think it's so hard to believe memories?

For a number of reasons:

It's less painful to believe you made it up than to believe people who loved you could do terrible things. It would make you question whether they really loved you and what that means about your lovability.

Believing also goes against years of reinforcement from others of the notion that what was happening was not really happening. If your childhood environment had been one that acknowledged the abuse as wrong, it would have been stopped. Since it wasn't stopped, the environment had a strong bias that you, as a child, were required to buy into. Everyone had to pretend that all was normal. Now, in order to believe the reality of what actually happened, you are having to disbelieve what you were taught then. It's hard.

Did you do anything to try to "prove" your memories?

I never intentionally tried to prove them. But, certain things have happened that have validated them. For example, my stepsister told me of an incident with the family employee who had raped me. She was a teenager. He was still working for my family (this would have been several years after he raped me). She went upstairs in our restaurant and encountered him there. He had been drinking. He grabbed her and tried to force himself on her. She was able to get away from him. This helped me believe that someone I trusted really did rape me.

What if your stepsister hadn't shared her own experience with you? How crucial was that in your recovery? If a survivor can't get any external validation, does that matter?

Great question. Many survivors will never get external validation. In fact, many will face angry denial from everyone involved. Truth is truth, period. It does not require validation. The *only* thing that matters is recovering your truth. You are the only one who gets a vote about what happened in your own life. Do not give others the power to override your truth.

There has been a lot of stuff in the press about people recovering memories and later recanting their claims of abuse. What do you think of that?

It's a good question and I don't have a good answer. I don't know the circumstances or the people involved. All I can speak to is my personal experience. None of the incest survivors I know have ever come to believe that their memories are not true. And never once in my survivor group did I doubt that someone was telling the truth. You know truth when you see the raw pain in a survivor's face as they talk. You know the truth behind the tears and the fears. It's there and it's real. You just *know* it.

YOUR ACTION

Your action around believing is to come back to this list whenever you are questioning your memories. Ask yourself:

- Why did I buy this book? If nothing happened to me, why would I have picked this book out of millions of other books?
- How is it serving me to have made this up?
- Am I questioning my truth out of fear of what will happen to relationships in my family? With my abuser?
- Do I need someone who has seen my pain to validate my truth? (This was very helpful for me at times. When I just couldn't bear to believe it myself, it helped to talk to others who knew it was true from having worked with me. I turned to my incest survivors group and my therapist.)

Chapter 11

TELLING

Of all the dynamics within the incestuous relationship, perhaps the most powerful is the threat that keeps the child from telling others what is happening. When someone with tremendous power over a child threatens death if the child tells—or holds out some equally frightening "if/then" scenario—the child believes it will occur. And the threat never leaves, even in adulthood. Some part of the individual goes on believing that catastrophe awaits if the truth is revealed.

The irony at this point is that the bad stuff has already happened. Now the catastrophe is in the *not* telling.

MY STORY

As the memories started flowing and I pieced them together, the picture was pretty bad. I knew, intellectually, that I needed to share what had happened to me. I needed people who believed me. I had been alone with the pain for so long —it was time to let it out. The only way was to tell.

Since I had built a strong support system, I had safe people to tell. This was very important. Had I told the wrong person at first and he or she had questioned the truth of what I was saying, it could have set me back for a long time. I usually wrote down what had happened in my journal first. Then I would tell it to someone—either my husband or therapist. Then I would share it with my survivors group.

It's hard to describe the difference between how I felt inside the 30 seconds *before* I told versus the 30 seconds *after* I told. Before, every muscle in my stomach, chest, shoulders, throat and jaw was tied into knots. If I closed my eyes I could see a huge black, bottomless pit that I was about to fall into, never to return. And the child-voice in my head was screaming "No, no, no! Never, never tell!"

Here's where that leap of faith comes in. I told anyway. Bravest thing I've ever done in my life. And guess what? The world didn't end. Nobody died. And people *believed* me. They *knew* it was true. They could see it on my face. And the tightness in my body dissolved and was replaced by a warmth that flooded

49

me, comforted me. When I speak of the beauty of the healing process, here it is. To break a 30-year-old taboo. To tell. To speak the truth. It's a beautiful thing. I swear it is.

OUR WALK

What's so important about telling someone? Isn't it enough that you know yourself?

As a child, you were most likely alone with this. Those children who were able to tell someone who believed and stopped the perpetrator were rare and fortunate. Most of us had to be alone with it. Some of us suppressed the memory as it happened, yet knew on some level that something was terribly wrong. Others remembered it and lived with the awareness every day. Either way, it's a terribly lonely existence.

Healing demands that we not be alone with it any longer. This means that people other than we, the survivors, must know what happened. As children, we may not have had anyone with this awareness in our world, but we can have them now. This helps free us from our isolation. It validates our truth.

You told a lot of people. Why not just one or two?

Every time I told, I felt better. Stronger. Empowered. Validated. And, every time, it got easier. I also wanted those close to me to know my story. To understand me better. Telling those in my survivor group was really important, too. They had been through it. They were the ones who could do more than just believe me, they could *understand.*

When you talk about telling someone who is "safe," what do you mean?

"Safe" people are those you trust to be respectful of your truth. To take it seriously. To understand how important it is to you. And *never* to question that you are telling the truth. One of the leftover effects from the incest dynamic is the fear that we won't be believed. So, as we venture into telling, we need to tell people who will believe us.

"Safe" people are also those who can hear your truth without having a reaction that is really more about them than anything else. People who have abuse in their past may deny your truth because they are still denying theirs. And they may be rather coarse about it. It's hard to know in advance who they are. I made the mistake of sharing my truth with one of my best friends. I thought she would be safe because she had always been a very loyal, respectful friend. When I told her about being raped, she made a very crass joke about it. Very crass. Very, very painful. I never spoke of it to her again. I learned she wasn't safe. Years later she shared that she had always kept the secret of the times her uncle had molested her. Then I knew. I understood her behavior years earlier. She discounted my pain because she was not yet ready to face her own.

YOUR ACTION

Start small. Start by telling *yourself*—with the promise that you will not tell anyone else until you are ready. Respect your timing on this. (On the other hand, don't put it off forever. The sooner you are ready to tell, the better your life will feel.)

Get a journal. Write your truth.

When you are ready, pick one person you trust. Make it someone who has proven himself or herself over time. Set the parameters for the discussion. Tell the person what you want: a listening ear and, no matter what you say, belief that what you tell them is true. You do not want them to question the truth of what you say in any manner. Ask if the person can agree to these conditions in advance.

I know it is asking a lot of anyone to agree ahead of time to believe whatever you tell him or her. That is why these listeners must be chosen with great care. If you don't have anyone in your life that you can trust to do this, you will be safer sharing your truth with a trained professional like a therapist.

Over time, find others to tell. Tell as many times as you need to. Tell until you feel completely validated. The number of times you need to tell will be individual to you. (As I have said many times, you can't surpass incest survivors group for this. I once read that the only type of person who will be able to listen as much as you will need to talk is another survivor.) It's ironic that we will eventually talk endlessly about the truths we hid for so long.

Chapter 12

TELLING THE TRUTH TO THOSE WHO WERE THERE

The previous chapter was about telling "safe" people, which usually means objective people who were not involved in the abuse—and who quite possibly do not know anyone in your life from that time. That's clearly the best place to start. They weren't close to the situation, so it is easier for them to hear and accept. They have no agenda.

But, what about the people who *were* involved? For example, family members who did not commit the abuse but somehow have an emotional stake in the truth because they lived in the same environment in which the abuse occurred. Telling them can be really tricky. Here's why: They usually have a vested interest in maintaining the status quo. Maybe they knew and remained silent. Maybe they were abused themselves and aren't able to deal with it yet. Maybe they didn't know the details but knew that something was terribly wrong and took no action. Whatever their reasons, they were part of a secretive environment that conditioned them to silence. Your telling violates that silence. You never know how they will react.

So, don't tell them until you are ready. For me, this means don't tell until you are able to let the telling be about you, rather than about their reaction.

MY STORY

It had been coming on for months. Pressure building up inside. This insanity of owning what had happened to me as a child and interacting with my mother as if nothing had happened at all. As if my childhood had been ideal.

I had tried to confront her about it many times—but I could not get the words to come out of my mouth. What would it take? What was stopping me?

Good question. There were two obstacles.

First, I was afraid that my mother's lifelong denial, expressed through inaction and silence, would cause her to not believe me now. That would have been really hard for me to deal with. A survivor spends her/his childhood knowing something is terribly wrong, and everyone else in the household is acting as if all is very normal. That's why it's so hard to tell in the first place. You don't trust your own assessment of the situation. So, to finally dig out the secret and tell the truth, and then have someone you love tell you it's not true could be excruciating.

Second, I didn't want to hurt my mother. Whatever she said in response, there was no doubt that confronting her with the abuse would mean hurting her.

For a long time those reasons kept me silent, yet I was churning inside.

Eventually I came to understand that the only way I could do this scary thing—this confrontation—was to make it about me, not about her. In other words, I had to say the words just to say the words—and totally detach myself from her response. The purpose of confronting, for me, was to speak the truth. It wasn't to hurt her. It wasn't to lay blame. It was simply to tell the truth of my childhood to someone who had been there, and to say that what had happened was *not okay*. I had to say the words and know that I had gotten what I needed simply by saying them.

If I got caught up in pinning everything on whether she believed me, I could be setting myself up for disaster. The truth was, I had no idea how my mother would respond. I knew denial had been a powerful tool for her all her life, and it was likely to kick in now. I also knew from other survivors that most parents deny the truth when confronted. They often turn on the survivor, assigning blame or accusing her/him of lying.

In short, I couldn't evaluate the outcome of telling on whether or not my mother believed me. It had to be enough to simply say my truth, and count that as the victory.

Also, I couldn't protect her. Although I really didn't want to hurt her, and in fact, loved her very much, the time had come to put myself first. I was going to tell the truth even *if* it hurt her. The fact was, her pain would be a consequence of her own choices, not mine. I became very clear on that.

Finally, I did it. At the time we lived halfway across the country from each other, and I didn't want to wait, so I did it on the phone. I don't remember how I led into it. I remember telling her of the rape when I was ten years old. I waited. I couldn't breathe. I was really, really scared. But, it felt really good! Before I knew what her reaction was going to be—in that moment before I heard anything back—I knew I had done what I needed to do. No matter what happened next, I knew I was okay because I had told my truth, and it felt fantastic!

She wailed. It was a maternal, primeval cry. A sound I have never heard before or since. And it spoke volumes. It told me she believed me. It told me that, on some unconscious level, she knew all along. It was an affirmation. It was a release. It was an unexpected gift.

I have immense respect for how my mother handled my telling the truth of my childhood. She found the strength to believe me even if it meant facing pain she had unconsciously buried for years. She took the truth head on and owned it. No denial here. She said how sorry she was for not knowing. (I believe she really did not know on a conscious level.) She said how sorry she was that she didn't take better care of me, that she let me be so damaged.

This telling happened about ten years ago, and never once since then has she ever questioned the truth of what I know about my childhood. She has stood by me and believed me even when it was very hard for her to do. She has even been very supportive of my writing this book.

Here's the gift my mother gave me that day. She stood by me, as she had never been able to do when I was young. In that moment, her maternal instincts kicked in and she did what was best for her child. I had a mother again.

My mother's reaction allowed us to move forward in our relationship. I can be myself with her. I can tell the truth. I can respect her. And I know I am very lucky, because often this is not the way these revelations turn out. And, here's the really important part: Had her reaction been the opposite, had it been my worst nightmare, I still would have been glad that I confronted her. It really was about me telling my truth. That's where my true healing came.

OUR WALK

Why tell these people who can be so hard to tell? Why not just tell the "safe" ones?

Let me make this clear. There may be people you choose never to tell. It just won't be worth it to you. If they are really crazy or abusive themselves, not telling them is a legitimate choice. If they are at the end of their lives and you love them and know it would be devastating to them, you may decide not to tell them. There are a number of circumstances in which you may choose not to tell.

But, sometimes, it becomes too much to live in a divided world—the world where you have told your truth and feel really good about that, and the other world where you are still pretending nothing happened. For me, this dual existence came to be intolerable. I was no longer willing to pretend, with anyone, that what happened to me as a child didn't actually happen.

What do you mean about the telling being about you rather than about the other person's reaction?

You know the time is right to tell when your motive is *to tell the truth* simply for the sake of the truth. Period. Nothing else. When it is no longer about that person believing you, or feeling sorry for you, or apologizing. When getting a particular reaction is not your reason for telling, you are ready.

You also need to have enough of a support system in place so that it will not devastate you if the person has an undesirable reaction. If they go nuts and call you a liar, that won't feel good, but you will be able to understand that their reaction is all about them. It's not about you.

I don't understand how you can say that your mother had known all along, but that you also believed she didn't know on a conscious level. Please explain more about that.

I believe everyone who lives in an incestuous family environment knows something is wrong. Those who are not able to bring that knowledge to a conscious level employ a tremendous amount of denial. So, while my mother did not know on a conscious level, I believe a deeper part of her sensed that something was terribly wrong with her child. For her, it would have been too unsafe to let these concerns rise to the conscious level. So, in that sense, she didn't know a thing.

YOUR ACTION

The first action I want you to take is to decide if, at this point, there is anyone who was there whom you want to tell. If the answer is "no," honor your instincts about this. If, at a later point, you become conflicted about living in today's truth most of the time, but at other times feeling like you have to revert to the childhood burden of pretending nothing happened, then reconsider the matter of whom you wish to tell.

If you decide you want to tell someone who was there, then consider the following questions:

- What is my *real* reason for wanting to tell? If it has anything to do with getting a particular response from the person, or hurting the person, then you should probably wait until you have a different answer.
- What will I say?

- Is there anything I will request of them before I begin the discussion? (For example: "All I want you to do is listen. I am not asking for a response.")
- Is there anything they might say that would be damaging to me? If so, you might want to wait. Only you can decide what would be damaging to you at any point of your healing.
- When and where will I tell them?
- Would I like to have anyone there with me for support?

Chapter 13

CONFRONTING THE PERPETRATOR

At some point in healing, there comes a moment of decision. Confront the perpetrator or not? This is such a complex issue that I recommend working with a trained professional when making this decision.

The fact that someone is dysfunctional enough to abuse a child makes him or her an inherently unsafe person to confront. The individual has a vested interest in denial. And, through the incest, the person has set up a complicated web of intimidation with the survivor.

It's important to remember that you may choose from a couple of courses of action. You may confront the perpetrator directly. Or, if that would not be good for you or is impossible for some reason, you can confront a surrogate.

MY STORY

With four abusers, there's a lot of confronting to do. It took years. It took facing tremendous fear and walking straight into it. It took the help of my incest group and the therapists who led it.

Three of my abusers were dead by the time I recovered my memories. I had no choice but to confront surrogates—either people role-playing the abuser or objects I endowed with the attributes of the abuser for a period of time. Or, by writing them letters to speak my mind.

I began with the therapists in my incest group. One would play the abuser and the other would support me as I confronted her. It's amazing how real this feels. All the emotions are front and center: fear, anger, hatred, shame. This was some of the most powerful work I did because it allowed me to say all the things I needed to say in a way that was safe for me.

At other times I used objects that I could physically attack. The physicality of it was important. I still keep a set of therapeutic bats—made to hit things without damaging them—in my closet. Even today, when the need to confront, to tell the truth, to lash out arises I take the bats out and beat the hell out of something I deem to be the abuser. It always serves me well.

In some cases, I wrote powerful letters to give voice to all the pain and hatred I had been holding inside. Putting that energy into the universe felt very cleansing and empowering—even though the abuser wasn't alive to read the letter.

As I write this, one abuser is still alive. Up to this point, I have not chosen to confront him directly. He's getting old, so I will have to do it soon if I'm going to do it at all. For now, I have decided not to. The main reason is that I believe him to be a truly evil man. The others were highly dysfunctional, but I don't deem them evil. I believe this man is evil. A professional friend of mine has the opinion that he's a sociopath, meaning he lacks a conscience. The way he has lived his life says that is true. I don't believe I would benefit from confronting him. Actually, I don't want to give him the opportunity to try to hurt me again. And he would try. It's what he does.

I must admit feeling a bit conflicted about this decision. On one hand, I know how powerful the confronting experience has always been for me. On the other, I don't want to risk making myself feel vulnerable to him in any way. Although I sincerely doubt he could still exercise that power, the truth is, I don't have any way of knowing since I haven't dealt with him for so long. The only way to find out would be to take a risk I'm not yet ready to take. Will I ever be ready? I don't know. I stay open to the possibility.

OUR WALK

I don't see how you can get any satisfaction at all out of confronting a surrogate. Please explain.

A therapist could give you a clinical reason; I can just give you the practical affirmation that it works. I felt enormous relief and power from the confrontations with surrogates. It felt real, it felt scary, it felt difficult, it felt challenging. And afterwards, I felt strong and proud for having done it. Every time.

If you were going to confront the actual person, what steps would you take?

I would do the following things:
- Work with a trained professional to decide if this is the best course of action for you.
- Wait to confront until you know you will not be damaged by the abuser's reaction, no matter what he/she does.

- Decide what you want out of the confrontation. Plan what you will say. *Practice* it.
- Think about what reaction you might receive and how you might respond.
- Decide whether to have someone there for support during the confrontation.
- Pick the time and place that feel safest. If you have any concerns about a physical reaction from the abuser, bring enough people with you to ensure your safety.

You had four abusers. Is it common to have multiple abusers?

I don't know how common it is. In my situation, the dynamic that led to one abuser being in my life opened the door for many abusers. My mother was attracted to abusers. Because she didn't have a filter for who was safe and who wasn't, she allowed a lot of unsafe people into my world.

If I remember one abuser, should I be concerned that there were others?

Not necessarily. And I certainly wouldn't go looking for them. If there were others, they will surface when you are ready.

YOUR ACTION

You'll know when it's time to confront. Don't feel a need to rush. When you feel ready to deal with the decision, you can choose whether to confront the actual abuser or a surrogate. Work with a professional. This is an area in which you should make sure you get all the support you need.

Chapter 14

FROM VICTIM TO SURVIVOR

Once we come to understand the impact of abuse on our past, we often tell ourselves that we are victims. It's a common term. Victims of crime. Victims of rape. Victims of a disaster. Victims of sexual child abuse. Incest victim.

I hate the word "victim." It's powerless. It's passive. Again, I point to the passage from Eckert Tolle that opens this book. The world "victim" wrongly suggests that the past is more powerful than the present.

For we who make the choice to heal, the idea of victim simply is not relevant. At the moment of violation, one is a victim. But now we have a choice not to be. Those of us who have chosen to keep living are no longer victims. We are *survivors*.

I like that word. Survivor. It has power and action and energy.

Survivor means that you have made the choice not to let the abuse kill you. Or destroy your life. Or keep you down.

Survivor. Good word. Claim it. Use it.

MY STORY

I went from being a victim to a survivor when I read *The Courage To Heal* and first read the term "survivor" used for someone in my circumstances. Later, when I joined my incest survivor group, I came to appreciate the full meaning of the word. These women were no longer victims. They refused to live a shattered life. They had taken charge of their healing and were rebuilding. It took courage—amazing courage. I gained tremendous respect for the term "survivor."

In that group, for the first time in my life, I was in a place where I really belonged. I fit in. We all understood each other. I found a term, survivor, that made sense of my life. Once I knew I was an incest survivor, everything that had felt murky and dark began to come into the light and into focus.

Be proud that you are a survivor. Own your ability to survive. Know that it means you are special. Understand how strong you really are to have survived.

Someday, you will move beyond being *just* a survivor. Someday, you will round out your self-description with lots of wonderful terms that connote action, positive accomplishment and joy. But for now, wear the term "survivor" proudly. You've earned it.

OUR WALK

It seems that dwelling on the fact that you are an incest survivor is simply living in the past. Why would you want to do that?

I'm definitely not talking about living in the past. Claiming your identity as a survivor is very much about creating a different and better present and future. Survivors are very, very strong people who have overcome a lot to be where they are today.

As children, our sense of self is stolen when we are violated. Then, usually, those around us deny the abuse. We are told that what we know is real actually isn't real after all. We then begin to question our own reality.

Once we understand there was abuse in our past and that we survived it, we have something to hang our hats on. I know this might sound odd, but at a certain point in our life, it's a very important identity. Being able to claim "I am an incest survivor" matters enormously. Having a self-chosen and affirmed identity provides context for our lives, for why we are the way we are.

Claiming the survivor identity also begins to restore the sense of control that was lost during the abuse. You and I didn't have a choice about being abused. Now, we do have a choice. A choice for survival. Being a survivor is an empowering thing.

YOUR ACTION

Have you ever said the words, "I am an incest survivor?" If so, great. No more homework.

If not, try saying those words. Out loud. To yourself at first. Say it while looking in a mirror. Then try it with someone you trust—make sure the individual is someone who won't be negative or judgmental.

How do you feel when you say the words?

Over time, as you heal, you will be able to say them without a lot of effort. They will be easily spoken, like saying "I have blue eyes." At that point, you will be ready to move *beyond* the limited identity of incest survivor to the greater, more complete individual that is you. More about that later in this book.

Chapter 15

FRAME OF REFERENCE FOR "NORMAL"

Asure, confident sense of what is normal is one of the great robberies that incest and abuse inflict upon a child.

Whatever we grow up with is our norm. Without a way to compare what goes on in our homes with what goes on in other homes, incest survivors have no idea of the extent of dysfunction that existed in their childhood world.

MY STORY

One of my best friends and I were having dinner. For some reason I don't recall, the conversation turned to my telling her that when I was a child, a young man from Japan had worked for my family in exchange for a place to stay in the United States. I mentioned that I really liked the few months he was with us, because it meant I didn't have to live alone in the house.

As my friend questioned me, I told her that my mother and stepfather had moved into a different house on the same property. They left me to live alone, at age 12 or so, in the main house.

My friend is a pediatrician. Her jaw dropped. She was thinking of the impact this type of neglect would have on a child. Even more amazing to her was the fact that I had accepted my home life as totally natural—even after I became an adult. I had known her for years and had never thought to mention it. In fact, I had been in therapy for years and had never mentioned it there, either. I wasn't hiding anything, but I had no frame of reference to understand that parents just don't move out and leave a child to live alone.

When we have no frame of reference, we accept outrageous situations as normal. So it is with incest.

OUR WALK

I find it hard to believe that you were left to live alone as a child and you didn't find anything unusual about that? Didn't you notice that your friends all lived in the same house as their parents and you didn't?

Yes, I noticed, but I was so used to feeling different that it seemed normal. Nothing in my family seemed like my friends' families. I had been conditioned to just accept our unusual circumstances. My parents were divorced. My father was an alcoholic. My stepfather was a madman. All the sexual abuse was occurring, and I was forgetting it as it happened. Nothing in my world made any sense, and that began to feel *normal*. The fact that I lived alone at an early age was par for the course to me. This just shows how things can get incredibly out of whack when we don't recognize what is and is not normal.

Why is it important to develop a frame of reference for "normal" as an adult?

It puts things in perspective, so we can make choices *now* for a functional life. Without a frame of reference, we may perpetuate harmful patterns simply because we don't realize they are dysfunctional. A perfect example is the woman who marries an abusive man after living a childhood of abuse. It feels normal. There is no frame of reference for what living with a non-abusive man would be like.

What is the best way to develop a frame of reference?

For me, the best course was to talk with people who could validate what was "normal" and what wasn't. I had to be told some things over and over again. Like that it was not normal for me to be left alone many times with a 45-year-old man who had a history of alcohol abuse. Or that it was not normal for my stepfather to fondle me at night under the guise of checking my underwear under my nightgown.

What else helped you re-frame "normal"?

I was amazed to watch some of my friends with their children. They treated the kids respectfully. I had never seen that kind of parent-child interaction before. Their children were allowed to have an opinion. My frame of reference, at first, was so skewed that I thought the parents were just being soft. Over time, I came to realize that this is the way to raise healthy children.

Observing people whose lives worked well is a good way to re-frame. Look at how they do things, the choices they make, the way they treat others. I've already mentioned my husband's family as one illustration. Another example was my business partner. David was a great teacher in this respect. He had a very sound sense of who he was, with strong boundaries. He modeled this every day just in the way he conducted himself. Over time, I learned by watching him. His example helped me come to a new understanding of what was "normal".

YOUR ACTION

A great exercise for creating a frame of reference is to write your life story. It doesn't have to be a huge volume—just bullet points of key aspects of your life will suffice. Then share it with a therapist or members of your survivor group. Get their feedback. Have them validate for you things that were dysfunctional.

Now, look at your life today and ask yourself if you are perpetuating any of this dysfunction. Decide what changes you will commit to make. Begin taking action.

Chapter 16

FEELING THE FEELINGS

Healing is not an *intellectual* exercise. It's important to understand your life in the context of the abuse, of course, but eventually, healing comes down to feeling your feelings.

When abuse happens, the natural response is to feel a storm of emotions about the violation—anger, hurt, anxiety, shame, terror.

But, at the time of the abuse, we don't have the luxury of feeling such emotions fully. We need to survive. This often means stuffing what we are feeling—packing it away out of our mind's eye.

Prior to healing, we spend a lot of energy trying not to feel those stuffed emotions. We go numb. Or, the emotions spill out at times that are not appropriate for the situation. We use today's events to surface old emotions. And when this happens, we can seem like the proverbial "basket case" to people around us.

Here's the deal: Until you can feel your feelings about the original violation, your life isn't going to work very well.

MY STORY

My husband surprised me with a trip to the mountains. We went to a lovely bed and breakfast with gorgeous vistas of the autumn colors. We hiked the banks of a beautiful river. Ideal. Romantic.

I couldn't feel a thing.

I remember staring at that river and knowing that I should be appreciating the beauty of this day. Of this man who loved me so. Nothing. Absolutely nothing.

Shortly after that trip, I became aware of a concept that made a lot of sense to me: You can only feel joy to the degree that you are willing to feel pain. The trip to the mountains came at a point in my healing when I was avoiding feeling all the "bad" feelings. This kept me from feeling the joy in that trip to the mountains. My life felt like cardboard. I was unable to experience the joy that exists in all situations.

As I learned to open myself to my feelings, I became aware of a sense of joy that I had never known before. And a sense of love. And delight in simple things. Life filled with color, sounds, smells. A wonderment began.

It's worth feeling the feelings to claim the wonderment.

OUR WALK

Why is it important to dig up all this old pain? Why not just leave it alone and move on?

The old pain works as a chain that holds you in place until you unlock yourself from it. As long as you confine the emotional range within which you live, you will limit the joy you could be experiencing. Until you feel all your feelings, they stay stuck inside you and you stay stuck in your old patterns.

I don't know what you mean by "feel the feelings." Exactly how does someone do that? What if they are stuck inside? What if you don't even know what they are?

This is an important question. It is hard, after years of stuffing them, to suddenly say "Okay, now let's feel." Like so much else in this healing process, this work takes time.

Different techniques may help tap into our feelings.

You may notice times when you know you should be feeling something, but you aren't. For example, your boss has just done something disrespectful to you. You should be angry, but you feel numb. At such a moment, tune into your body. Is there a place those feelings seem to be stuck? (Does your chest feel tight, your back hurt, your throat feel constricted?) Ask your body what's stuck there and to let you feel it. Experience what comes up.

Or you may connect to your feelings by doing something physical like exercise or yoga. Or by getting a massage. Or being in a very relaxed state. My experience in the mountains notwithstanding, being in nature can sometimes connect us to our stuffed emotions.

Try different things and see what works for you. You'll know what works when your emotions flow rather than getting stuck in your body.

As I have said before, the setting is very important. You will need to have a safe environment in which to let these feelings out—a place where they (and you) will be honored.

What do you do with these feelings once you feel them?

You get them out any safe way you can! I remember a time a friend of mine (another incest survivor) and I were having a yard sale. She brought over a box that contained a full set of dishes she intended to sell. We were both very irritable with each other as we were preparing for the sale. We realized that it was "old stuff" bubbling up. It was anger about our incest and it needed an outlet.

We put the dishes in my car and drove to a place where the city was building a bridge and had installed huge concrete walls for support. No one was around. One by one, we smashed those dishes against the wall. We named them with our abusers' names. We named their crimes. We shattered them. We annihilated that entire set of dishes.

What power! What relief. What fun!

So the answer is to get it out. Whatever you are feeling. In any way you can. Cry it out. Scream it out. Break things (safely). Talk it out. Write it out. As someone once told me, there is a lot more room on the outside than on your insides. Let it out! Always be careful to deal with feelings in a way that will not harm yourself or others. If you have concerns about this, seek support from a therapist as you do this work.

What if it damages me to feel these feelings? I know I have been protecting myself by not feeling them.

When you were a child, you had to protect yourself by not feeling. You didn't have the support system in place to handle those emotions. As an adult, you have the ability to make it safe to feel them.

If you have concerns about letting the feelings out, work with a trained professional. He/she can help you know what is safe. My own experience is that I never felt something I wasn't ready to feel. Feeling my feelings never once damaged me.

How do you go about living a normal life with all these feelings pouring out all the time?

You feel the feelings and they pass. This is one of the ways you know that "freefalling" as I described it earlier is safe and healing rather than dangerous. The feelings don't stay with you in a heightened state forever. Once they pass, you usually feel a sense of relief. Then, you are able to get back to your normal life.

YOUR ACTION

As with most of the concepts in this book, feeling your feelings is not a one-time deal. You will come back to this over and over again.

First, recognize that—as I have said before—feelings are *just* feelings. As you "un-stuff" them, they lose their power over you. In fact, feelings can remind you that the power is now in your hands. *You* get to decide what, if any, action to take when you feel something.

Second, remember that if you resist feeling a feeling, that feeling becomes stronger. You have to spend more effort to keep it in. On the other hand, if you move toward it, rather than shy away from it, it will intensify for a while and then diminish. It goes away!

Try this when you think you are ready:

- See if you can identify one feeling (anger, sadness, shame, etc.) that is scary to feel.
- Is there a place it's located in your body?
- What are the characteristics (dense, hot, pressure, tight, etc.) of the feeling?
- Explore what happens if you simply observe it without becoming emotional about it. For instance, simply think "my neck feels tight" in a matter-of-fact way.
- When you are ready, move your focus toward it. Name it. "This is anger." "This is hatred." "This is shame." Open yourself to feeling it. Stop all resistance to it. Own it.
- Do anything physical (non-harming, of course) you need to do to let it out. Cry. Scream. Throw rocks! Whatever it takes. Or write it out, if that feels right.
- Notice what happens when you fully allow the feeling to surface and pass through you. How does your body feel after the feeling has passed? Doesn't it feel better than before?

Chapter 17

SHAME

It wasn't your fault. Know that. No matter what happened, when an adult chooses to be sexual with a child—or a teenager—it is not that child's fault. Period. Ever.

Please understand this! No matter what your abuser or an enabler has told you. No matter how you participated. No matter if you felt pleasure. No matter what. It was not your fault. Not in any way. Ever!

The shame we carry after incest is one of the most insidious aspects of the violation. It permeates our being and drives us to run away from ourselves. It makes us believe we are not worthy of relationships with good people. More than anything else, it keeps us silent.

MY STORY

I was a teenager and it was an innocent first date. He was a polite boy. A good boy. He held my hand as we walked around town. We had fun dancing. He kissed me good night when he took me home.

I felt dirty.

The shame I had been storing for so long was unleashed that night. And I ran from it for the next 18 years. It caused me to slide into deep depression if I became still enough to feel. I wanted to do anything but to be with myself. I became numb to myself in countless ways. As a result, I sabotaged good relationships and came close to losing my husband.

Linda was one of the two therapists running the incest survivor group I joined. Of all the people who helped guide me through my healing, I trusted what she said the most. Linda has a rich, deep voice and gives the best hugs in the world. I'll never forget the day she wrapped me in her arms and said the words "Sweetie, it was not your fault." I knew she really meant it. And I started to believe it was true.

OUR WALK

How did you get over believing that you had been at fault somehow?

I did a number of things over and over again for a long time. Here are some things to try:

- *Literally hear it.* Have people you trust tell you it wasn't your fault. There is something very validating about hearing the words spoken by another person. By lots of other people.
- *Say it out loud.* Hear your own voice speak it. Even if you don't believe it yet, say it. Say it a million times. Say it until you believe it.
- *Read books by experts on child sexual abuse.* Any expert on incest will tell you it is never the child's fault.
- *Write it to your Inner Child.* Part of the Inner Child work I did was to have my Adult write to my Inner Child and tell her that it was not her fault. Eventually my Child was able to write it herself. Eventually she believed it. Eventually. (See the chapter on Inner Child work.)

What else did you do to get rid of the shame?

I told people about what had happened to me. At first it was really hard to get the words to come out. But every time I shared my story, I felt tremendous relief. And I knew I had worked through another part of the shame. The more I told, the less shame I felt. After a lot of telling—I mean *tons* of telling—a different feeling replaced the shame. It was a feeling of pride. Pride in my strength. Pride in my dogged determination to heal. Pride in that precious little child who somehow managed to survive years of violation. Pride feels a lot better than shame.

YOUR ACTION

Start paying close attention to how you are feeling and how you are acting. Find the shame hiding behind feelings and actions. Give it a name. Call it forth.

Every time you feel shame or suspect it is lurking, look at the list above and pick something to try. See what works. This won't be hard, because once you release just a little bit of shame, it feels so good you will want to do it often.

Also, it's important to avoid people who—for their own reasons—try to shame you. You just don't need that influence as you strengthen your resolve to release your shame.

Chapter 18

RAGE

This chapter is called "Rage" rather than "Anger" because I believe that anyone who has experienced sexual child abuse has a lot of rage inside. Rage is a natural response to a very unnatural violation. Most survivors handle their rage in one of two ways. Either they are angry all the time—sometimes violently so—or, they stuff it deep inside and never let it seep through. Either way, it eats them alive.

I think most survivors, on a deep level, are afraid of their rage. Over time I have come to understand that rage is just rage—no more, no less. And we need to let it out. Constructively! Rage can become our ally, believe it or not. And it can fuel massive healing and positive change. We need to learn how to harness it.

MY STORY

In spite of an impulse to take care of other people, I was a very angry person most of my life. Very Type A, fly off the handle, rage always simmering just below the surface. I was always mad at someone or something. It was usually disproportionate to what was really going on. This simmering rage was also effective in keeping people far enough away that they wouldn't hurt me. It was my mode of interface with the world. And, of course, it was killing me.

Given how practiced I was with my anger, you would think that when I delved into the healing process I would have had no trouble processing the anger stuffed inside. Wrong! This was the biggest stumbling block I hit.

I had no trouble being angry at little things in my life. But I absolutely could not feel the anger about my abuse. On an intellectual level, I knew I *must* be mad. But, to feel it—or to *say* it—no way! I could not say the words. I could not feel the feelings. I had stored them away so deep inside that it took a lot of digging to access them.

Here's what it took. I asked someone in my survivors group to be angry for me. I needed her to feel my anger and say it out loud. She was amazing. What a huge gift she gave me that day. She made it safe for me to do what was never safe for me to do as a child: feel and speak how I felt about the injustice. Finally, *finally,* it came spilling out. I got mad. I got physical (safe stuff, padded bats, etc.) and I got vocal. And, this time, I had witnesses to support me. I could be mad as hell, I could rant and rage. People cheered! What a moment!

Let me tell you something—experiencing your rage over what you are *really* mad about is so powerful. It absolutely sets your soul on fire—in a good way!

Finding my anger and letting it out appropriately was *the* turning point in my healing process. Once I was able to do that, I knew I would be okay.

Did you hear what I just said? Once I got in touch with my anger and learned to use it constructively *I knew I would be okay!* This was huge.

For the first time, I was engaged in *more* than a leap of faith. I knew. From then on, I started seeing results in my life. There was no doubt I was on the right path.

Before this episode of authentic anger, I had never written anything about my feelings before. On February 10, 1994, I wrote this:

MY ANGER

My anger fills the oceans
and laps the shores of all humanity.

My anger is the red of a thousand sunsets,
of hot air balloons, of blood.

My anger is the lava of earth's volcanoes
and spills over into all of my life.

I taste it on my lips.
Thick, bitter, salty.

I embrace it. A sword.
A shield. A laser.

I befriend it. It becomes
my power, my strength, my passion.

I release it. And harness it.
It flows through me like blood.

It becomes my friend.

My sentry. My protector. My champion.

My anger is a beam of pure, white light.
It shines into the darkness of my soul and sets me free.

It is my anger. And at last,
it is beautiful.

OUR WALK

Why was it so hard for you to reach your anger about the incest? It seems like that is the first feeling that would come up.

As a child, I couldn't safely own my anger. There were too many controlling, raging, dangerous people around me. It was clearly in their best interest that my anger never surface—because if it had, the truth of the incest would have surfaced with it.

Therefore I never developed the skill to process my anger. It just sat inside me like a dense, hot ball of fire. And it spilled out at times unrelated to my *real* anger. I knew how to be angry—I didn't know how to be angry about the incest.

How do you ever let ALL the anger out? I don't think there would ever be an end to it if I let it start flowing.

You let it out a chunk at a time, for a long time. And I don't know if it ever runs out, since I still feel it occasionally. When I do, I find a way to release it. What once was so hard has become second nature. I brushed my teeth today. I processed some anger. It becomes commonplace. Over time, the volume and rate of flow has slowed down considerably. For a long time I felt a lot of anger. Now it's just every now and then.

Doesn't the anger eat you up as you feel it?

No. As with all feelings, anger only eats you up when you *don't* feel it. When you let it flow, it's cleansing and healing.

I don't have any problem feeling my anger. I'm mad as hell at my abuser. I'm so mad I can't think of anything else.

79

Great! That is, as long as you are using the anger for your benefit. Take a close look at whether you are letting the anger flow constructively. Look at whether it spills over into current situations or if it is confined to the original source. Look at whether it burns you. Look at how you can be using it most productively.

I don't understand what you mean about using anger productively. How can you use a negative emotion productively?

There was a period of time when I was feeling a lot of anger toward my father. This anger felt so big that I wasn't sure what to do with it. As I checked in with myself, my sense was that I needed to do something physical. I took on the massive project of building a large box garden on my deck. I did the whole thing myself. Hauled the lumber. Drilled the holes. Heaved countless bags of peat moss and manure. Dug and mixed and watered the soil. For day after day, I sweated and grunted out that anger.

That's using anger constructively. By the time I was finished with that garden, my anger was depleted. Better still, I was left with something that for years has given me a gift of beauty with each new season.

YOUR ACTION

When you are ready, make contact with your anger. As always, find a safe place. Ask yourself:

- What do I need to do or say to (safely) give voice to my anger?
- What does my body need?
- Do I need a witness? Lots of witnesses?
- Where in my body is it stuck?
- What will it take to loosen it and let it flow?
- Can I be with my anger and stay unafraid?
- Am I willing to honor it as an appropriate, healthy response?
- Is there a way to use it productively?

You will probably need to come back to this exercise time and again.

And remember, there's always more room on the outside than on your insides!

Chapter 19

DISMANTLING

MY STORY

I am a person of strong values and high integrity. Anyone who knows me well will tell you that. In large part, I came to learn my ethics from my father. My dad was a good man. It has taken me years to be able to say this, but he was. That's why it was so hard for me to believe that he was a child molester.

My dad was also a very sick man and an alcoholic. And in his sickness he was terribly confused about love and power and sex. Hard to reconcile such extremes, you know—a good man and a child molester.

I loved my dad. He protected me from my stepfather. The world I lived in with my stepfather was a very dangerous one. He was a madman—terribly, overtly abusive. So, my dad felt safe by comparison. How could I ever believe, as a child, that what my dad was doing to me was wrong? How could I believe that my protector was also my abuser?

For months a scene had been intruding into my mind. Flashing without warning. Coming for no apparent reason. It was the beginning of an emerging memory. I was terribly afraid of it.

The scene in my mind was simple. It was of a black wrought-iron stairway against a brick wall. I knew where it was. It was halfway across the country in Houston. I climbed this stairway every time I went to my father's apartment as a child after my parents divorced.

But as my mind's eye saw the scene, there was something amiss in it. The angle of view was off. Remembering how the apartments were laid out, I couldn't imagine where I could have been standing to have that particular angle of view. It seemed physically impossible—as if I would have to have been floating in air between two apartment buildings.

The image simply wouldn't go away. Over and over I saw this stairway from the strange angle. It haunted me. I knew it would lead to another piece of the puzzle of my past. I was terrified, because I knew it was about my father.

I decided to do what, in retrospect, was one of the bravest things I've ever done. With my husband, I went to Houston. We drove to my father's old neighborhood and found the apartment complex. I sat in the parking lot thinking about whether I could do what I had come to do. The entire experience was surreal.

We got out of the car and walked to his old building. There it was. The stairway. But from the wrong angle. Where could I have been when I saw the angle in the image? Paul and I climbed up the stairs. There was my father's old apartment. There was the door. The window. His hand had touched that doorknob. A chill ran down my spine.

I had to find the angle of view in my memory. We walked downstairs again and up the stairs of an adjacent building. Again, not quite the right angle. Then it hit me. The only place I could have been to see the stairway from that particular angle was looking out the window of the apartment next to my father's. The physical impact of this realization was incredible. I said to my husband, "Paul, feel my skin." I had broken out in a cold sweat. I was drenched. My heart was racing. I felt frozen in place.

It came back over time, this memory of my father. It was horrible. I was six years old. I had been swimming all afternoon in the pool. My father had been drinking a lot. He said it was time to go back to his apartment. We did. I was in my bathing suit. He started talking nonsense. He scared me. He was getting mad. He cornered me in the dressing room and pushed me against the wall. He began to force himself on me. I tried to get away, but he was six feet tall and I was six years old. I was trapped and horrified.

Suddenly, I felt his weight leave me. He started to get sick and ran into the bathroom. I ran out of the apartment, pulling my bathing suit up. I banged on the door next to my father's. Relief flooded me when a woman opened the door. I told her that my father had been drinking and that I needed to call my mother to come get me. She let me use her phone. I dialed my mother's number. It rang and rang. My mother was not home. The hopelessness of the situation pierced me like a knife.

The woman didn't know what to do with me. I asked her if I could stay there until my mother came home. She said I could. I went to the window and knelt on the bed under it. I put my chin on the windowsill. That's where I stared at the stairway. Stared at it until that was all there was in my world. Stared at it until the horror of the afternoon could be forgotten.

A sudden, hard knock sounded on the door. It was my father. He was clean and straight talking. He admonished me for bothering this lady and said it was time to come home. I had no choice. I went back with him. Then I forgot everything that happened and didn't remember it for the next 30 years.

Accepting incest as a part of my past meant dismantling the story I had told myself about my life. It meant seeing people as they really were, not as I had wanted them to be. It meant knowing that the people I loved had hurt me deliberately. It meant accepting that my mother, whom I treasured, had left me unprotected with unsafe people. It meant acknowledging that many of the men I trusted had misused their power over me.

This rocked my world.

For a while, it felt like everything I ever believed in had been shattered. And it pretty much had. I remember feeling like I had been gutted—ripped apart with nothing left inside. I felt like there was absolutely nothing I could believe in. I said this one night in our survivor group. One of the therapists asked me if there was *anything* I could say was true. I couldn't think of one thing. She said "What about that the sun will rise in the morning and set in the evening?" Yes. I could believe in that.

It was a beginning.

OUR WALK

Why do you use the word "dismantling"? Seems like an odd choice of words.

For me, "dismantling" means to consciously take apart the myths we once needed to survive. They are not serving us well now. And we can't move forward very far while they are still in place. It means taking down the old structure of survival, built on unconscious denial and avoidance of feelings, to have clean ground on which to build the healthy new structure of our future.

Did you really do it consciously? Sounds more like it just happened to you.

It *felt* like it just happened to me, but as I look back, I made decisions every day to look at certain myths and decide whether to carry them forward.

Tell me more about the "myths" you mentioned.

One myth was that my father was my protector, the one I could really trust. The truth was that my father was a very sick man. He was an alcoholic—something that no one in the family ever identified as a problem. He focused on his relationship with me when my mother divorced him. What I thought was protection was actually his way of taking care of himself. He looked to his daughter inappropriately for the kind of relationship he should have found with mature women. My father sexualized his relationship with me after he and my mother divorced.

Another myth was that my mother was my protector. In many ways, she was a good mother. She always let me know how much she loved me. We had many close times together. But she didn't protect me. She was so absorbed in her issues that she was not vigilant relative to her daughter. She lived in denial a lot of the time because of the very abusive relationship she was in with my stepfather. Many times she traded my security for peace with him. Bad trade off for me.

I had protected my parents by going along with the myth that they were my protectors, fulfilling that part of their job as parents. In order to move on, I had to look at those myths directly, dismantle them, tell the truth to myself and eventually to the world.

So once you decided to not carry on with a myth, what did you do?

I told myself the truth. This was usually through journaling or talking to my therapist or in group. It's important that as you dismantle your survival structure, you do it in a way that doesn't leave you high and dry. So, I did it in the presence of others who would help support me while I rebuilt.

I'm really put off by the fact that you say your father was both a good man and a child abuser. How can you assert that one person can be both? Sounds to me as if you still believe the myth.

I respect your position. And I understand it. In fact, I held that same position for years. When I remembered what my father had done to me, I could only see him as all bad. That felt right to me for a long time. But eventually something in that thinking felt out of line. I knew he had a sense of integrity that he had passed on to me. I knew there were times he was genuinely kind and loving. He wasn't evil like my stepfather. He was sick. He did horrible things. I had to piece him together for my own sake, reclaiming the parts of my father that I loved and that had been good for me. I had to tell the whole truth.

I still don't buy it.

That's okay. I understand. It's a tough question, "Can someone who is a child abuser also be a good person?" I encourage you to revisit this question over time and notice if your answer changes at all.

YOUR ACTION

STEP ONE: On a piece of paper, draw a line down the middle to make two columns. On the left hand side, make a list of all the myths that have been part of your survival structure. Write this list knowing that you don't have to give up any of the myths until you want to.

STEP TWO: Go to the right hand column. For each myth, describe what new support would have to be in place for you to let go of that myth.

Example: I had a myth that my mother protected me. In order to dismantle the myth, I had to create a safe place for myself as an adult that did not depend on her protection. Then I could let go of the myth and tell the truth: While my mother was a very good mother in many ways, she allowed me to be with dangerous people and either didn't notice or didn't respond to the changes in me when I was suffering so terribly.

STEP THREE: Once you have new support in place for an old myth, write the truth about that myth.

STEP FOUR: Let go of the myth. This may take time. You may need to let go of it over and over again.

Part Two: Creating a Great Future

Chapter 20

BUILDING A NEW FOUNDATION

MY STORY

So I knew the sun would rise in the morning and set in the evening. It was a good start. It was the beginning of my new foundation.

Slowly I began to put my world back together. Actually, it was more like putting it together for the first time. Everything I believed in had been shattered. There wasn't much to build on, I thought. But then I found something.

Deep inside, I found *me*! I discovered that core of my being which had been strong enough to survive. There was someone home!

Plus, that someone had a set of positive assets to put to work. There were certain survival skills I had acquired as a defense mechanism against the abuse. Now, they would serve me well by helping me rebuild my life.

For example, I had "radar" —the ability to walk into a situation and read it instantly.

I also had a quick mind and a strong instinct for self-protection. In addition, I had a support system that had been missing for many years: a loving husband, some very good friends, a therapist and an incest survivor support group.

With these strengths, assets and tools, I was ready to build my future.

A valuable step was to read books to help me heal myself. Through study and learning, I worked diligently at becoming emotionally healthy.

I became aware of the choices I was making and whether or not they were working for me. One choice that was *not* working was that with regard to people, I sometimes let my head overrule my instincts. This was always a mistake. So instead, I started to trust my "gut" about people. After making some mistakes on this, I finally got it—my gut is *never* wrong. Not ever. Once I understood this, I had a very valuable tool for decision-making.

As a consequence, I replaced abusive people with healthy, supportive people. What a difference that made!

Not surprisingly, trusting men was an issue. I made a list of those men in the world I knew I *could* trust. There were five. For years, there were only five. So, I learned how to be with these five healthy men. Eventually I expanded my range. And, over the years, I have come to have many wonderful men in my life.

I rebuilt my relationship with my mother. On my terms. With strong boundaries. It was good for me. It was also good for her. We both grew. We built a real relationship.

As I took these steps, my life began working for the first time.

Then in 1998, I discovered the profession of coaching. Thomas Leonard, the father of today's professional coaching industry, had put together many amazing concepts for living an effortless life—a life of joy and fulfillment. As I studied to become a coach, I began living these principles. They work. As a result, my life works. My life has transformed from ruins to a life of utter joy.

Know this—the same is possible for you. You can make your life be what you choose. It takes time. It takes effort. You *can* do it!

OUR WALK

You make it sound so easy. Read a few books, rebuild a few relationships, live a great life. When you are standing where I am—where nothing in my life is working—that seems impossible.

So, first of all remember that it seemed impossible for me, too. It really did. For a long, long time. And I don't want to oversimplify or trivialize the journey in any way. It's a long passage with lots of hard work. What I do want you to know is that you *can* build a life beyond your wildest expectations.

I need more specifics. Exactly what did you do?

I did all the things I have talked about in this book. So far, those things have focused mainly on resolving the past. I also did the other things I am going to present in the next few chapters that allowed me to create the future.

Healing and making a great life is a twofold process:

RESOLVING THE PAST
+
CREATING THE FUTURE

As previously noted, it's not a linear process; however, a certain amount of resolving the past is necessary before you can move into creating the future. Be careful not to get ahead of yourself, but move at the pace that is right for you.

So what is this "Creating the Future" about?

For me, it's about all the things I learned from Thomas Leonard and from my training at Coach U. It's about understanding your needs and getting them met in a healthy way. About setting appropriate boundaries and enforcing them. About having standards by which you live. About eliminating things in your life that drain your energy. About orienting your life around those things that are the truest expression of who you are and why you are on this planet.

YOUR ACTION

Your action is simple. Look through the chapters of this section of the book and become familiar with the concepts. Ask yourself which concepts would be helpful to you at this stage of your healing. Give one a try and see how your life shifts. Keep coming back to these concepts. It's a life-long process.

Please note: The concepts presented in the upcoming chapters vary in their sophistication. You may be ready to apply some today. For others, it may take years before you are ready to put them into practice. Everything depends on where you are in your healing process. If you are in the Emergency Stage, that's probably all you can deal with at the moment. If you have worked through many of the things necessary to resolve the past, you may be ready to tackle a number of these future-oriented concepts.

Listen to what you need and follow your gut about when you are ready for what.

Chapter 21

THE ADULT AND THE INNER CHILD

Journal Entry:

Dear Inner Child,
I can sense that you are feeling out of sorts. I want to write and check in. Can you tell me how you are feeling?

I don't know.

Okay. Well, can you get real still and quiet and listen inside? What do you feel in your body?

My chest feels tight when I breathe. And my hands are sweaty.

So, can you tell me what feeling is causing that?

I guess I'm afraid.

I think you are, too. What do you suppose you might be afraid of?

That you told Janet we can't be friends anymore.

That's probably very scary for you isn't it? Do you know why?

No.

Because Janet is abusive and you were taught not to talk back to abusers because they would really hurt you.

So will Janet hurt us?

No, I won't let her. Because things are different now. You have me, the Adult. I'm here and very capable. I'm in charge of making the decisions that will keep you safe. You don't have to be in charge anymore. I'm here now.

And you won't let Janet hurt us?

Absolutely not. I'm here to take care of you. And if that means that some people can't be in our life, then that's the way it is. I want you to look to me for what you want, not to Janet. I'm the one you can trust. You weren't taken care of by Mother or Daddy, so you kept looking for someone to take care of you. You are still doing that. That's why you want Janet to be your friend. The problem is, Janet is abusive. I know she feels normal to you—because you learned that abusive behavior is normal, but it's not. So, I made the decision that Janet had to go. It's okay. You can look to me for protection now. I love you and I'm here to take care of you always.

MY STORY

Karen, my therapist, tossed out a strange concept in the middle of one of our sessions. "I know this sounds crazy, but I want you to think of yourself as having two parts. One part is the little girl who was hurt so badly at an early age. The other is the strong, capable adult you have grown to be. Let them get to know each other. Build a relationship between the two. Have them talk to each other."

I thought she was nuts. But I was pretty desperate at that point. So in the car on the way home I started talking to my "Inner Child." That is, my "Adult" talked to her. It was very awkward at first. And I felt pretty silly having this conversation with myself sitting in traffic.

Sometimes you have to feel a little crazy to get sane. That's what this Inner Child work felt like to me—splitting myself in parts and having them talk to each other. My Adult started out by saying "So, what's up with you?" and my Inner Child said "I'm sort of scared." And so began a lifelong conversation. It felt *very* odd at first.

Yet, this work became the *foundation* of building the future. It helped me understand the different—and often conflicting—parts of myself. It gave me a new way to heal and grow. A number of people in my incest survivor group used the technique, as well. It gave us a common language to explain what was going on to each other.

It came slowly. It took months to get used to the process. My Adult wasn't fully developed. It took time for her to come into her own. And my Child was used to running the show, because that was the only way she felt safe. Over time, my Child started testing what it would feel like to *not* have to run the show. To let the Adult run things and let the kid be a kid.

Together, they worked out how things would work in my life. The Adult is responsible for all major decision-making (with the Child's best interest the priority). This means decisions relative to what is safe and what is not. What is in the Child's best interest and what isn't. The Child is responsible for feeling and for telling the Adult what she (the Child) needs at any given time. For example, the Child might need to feel safe or to have fun or to rest. The Adult honors the Child's feelings and needs and creates a safe environment for her.

Early on, I incorporated this dialogue between these two parts into my journaling. My Inner Child and Adult have filled scores of journals over many years. And they have come to know each other *really* well.

Through this process, I have given myself the kind of parenting I wish I had received. Even now, as a highly functioning person, I continue this work. It keeps me in touch with *me*. And it feels *great!* It is by using Inner Child work that I have taught myself to look inward for validation, not outside. My Child looks to my Adult for validation, instead of to other—possibly unhealthy—people. It was my path to love. We all know we have to love ourselves before we can receive love from others. This was my way of loving myself. And *liking* myself. All of myself—the Adult and the Child.

OUR WALK

How did you learn to use this process?

At first, I just sort of made it up with the little bit Karen mentioned in that session. Then I started formally learning more about it. I went to a workshop given by John Bradshaw. He had just written a book called *Homecoming: Reclaiming and Championing Your Inner Child*. It is a book I recommend as an excellent way to learn about this work.

In the workshop, he took us through a meditation where we went back to our childhood home and met our Inner Child. We spent time with her and asked her if she would like to come away with us. She said good-bye to her parents and we carried her away. We brought her home with us and began a new life. It was very, very powerful. After the meditation, I actually felt like I had rescued my

Child and brought her to a safe placed to live with me. For the first time, my Child began to feel like things might be okay.

Tell me more about using journaling with Inner Child work.

Before I started doing Inner Child work, I was using a journal. The process was simple, I just wrote about what was on my mind. When I added the dimension of writing between my Adult and Inner Child, it became a hundred times more powerful.

The way I do it is I have my Adult start out by asking my Inner Child a question. Then, without thinking or editing, my Inner Child writes back. I use a process called alternate-hand writing. My Adult writes with my left hand (I am left handed) and my Child writes with my right hand (my non-dominant hand). I learned of this process from John Bradshaw. He didn't develop it, and I don't remember whom he credited with it.

Why do you have your Inner Child write with your non-dominant hand?

Because it seems to tap into the *feeling*, rather than *thinking* part of me. It's also very much like a child would write. When children first begin to write, it's awkward. They write slowly. It even looks like child's writing.

What kind of questions do you ask?

They are usually pretty simple. Like, "So, I can tell that you are feeling pretty shut down. Can you tell me what feelings are behind that?" Or, "We have the whole day to ourselves. What would feel good to you? What are you needing today?"

It's interesting. At first, my Inner Child had a hard time answering a question like "What do you need?" Her needs had never been important to anyone. Suddenly she was being asked what she needed and she was not in the habit of being in touch with what that might be. It took practice. For example, if the Child needed to feel safe, the Adult might probe further to understand exactly what would feel safe. Then the Adult would do what was necessary to create safety for the Child. Sometimes, the Adult would have to work out what the Adult needed as well as what the Child needed, if those needs conflicted in some way.

How often do you write in your journal on "Inner Child" stuff versus other things?

That depends on what's going on in my life. When I was going though a lot of memory recovery, I wrote often—several times a day if that's what it took. Now I write several times a month, more often when I need or want to. For many years, the Adult and Inner Child writing was what I focused on. More recently, I have returned to the more traditional method of journaling as well. Which method I use depends on my needs at the time.

I write between my Adult and Inner Child whenever

- I feel confused
- I am upset
- I want to celebrate a victory
- I feel out of touch with myself
- Something is out of sorts in one of my relationships
- I want to connect more strongly to my Inner Child
- I'm depressed and want to know what's behind it
- I need to figure something out
- I am about to make a big decision
- I am setting goals

YOUR ACTION

Start building a relationship between your Adult and your Inner Child. Here are the ground rules I suggest you follow:

- Think of how you would treat a small child coming to you after being hurt. Treat your Inner Child that way.
- Everything the Adult says to the Child will be unconditionally supportive.
- Always accept, without judgment, all the Child's feelings.
- The Adult makes all the major decisions—after hearing the Child's input.
- The Adult is the Child's champion. The Child's best interests *always* come first. The Adult decides what is in the best interest of the Child.

Try the alternate-hand writing technique in your journal as a way of dialoging between these two parts of yourself. Do this every day for a week and see how it feels. If it is useful, make it a standard part of your healing process.

There are a number of good books on Inner Child work. Go to Amazon.com and search for "Inner Child" and pick one that feels right for you. I highly recommend the Bradshaw book listed in the Recommended Reading section at the end of this book.

Chapter 22

ASSESSING YOUR SURVIVAL SKILLS

The human ability to survive deserves tremendous respect. Sitting week after week in incest survivor group and hearing the stories, I asked myself "How did she ever make it though that?" Children who survive incest develop some really strong survival skills. These skills have helped us navigate deadly waters. They served us well. In many ways, they shaped who we are.

Now, as adults, the crisis is over. And we still have—and use—these tools. Sometimes they give us an advantage in life. Many times they don't serve us as well now as they did in childhood—and may even get in the way of our happiness. It's time to examine the tools in our survival toolbox, and whether they are still serving us today. Are we using them well? Or, have they become a hindrance, perhaps even our worst enemy?

MY STORY

I call it "radar." It's an ability of mine to walk into a room and "feel" what's going on before anyone ever speaks a word. Or to walk into a house and know if someone is in it before I see or hear them. Or to know if what's true about a situation is not what people are saying is true. I perfected this skill as a child because I needed to be able to come home and know the lay of the land *before* it revealed itself.

With the help of my radar, I became an astute businesswoman at a very early age. Many of my instincts about business were linked to this tool. It serves me well still. I think I'll keep it.

Another survival tool was to maintain distance. If I don't let you get close, you can't hurt me. So I stay just out of reach. This ability led me to learn countless distancing skills. Anger is a big one. So is my inclination to suddenly lose interest if a relationship moves towards intimacy too quickly.

Today, no one hurts me. My intimate relationships have been carefully picked and tested over time. I'm certain that my distancing skills have kept me away from many abusive people, yet I'm equally certain I've missed opportunities to be close to some wonderful people. Sometimes I am lonely.

These distancing skills don't always serve me well. Time to see if I need to retire them.

OUR WALK

I've never thought that anything from the abuse could actually be an asset. What are some other skills survivors may have gained as a result of the abuse experience?

This varies by the individual, of course, but I have noticed the following traits in many of the survivors I have known. (As has been true for me, sometimes these skills work well for other survivors, and sometimes they work against them.)

- The ability to keep people away with no more than a facial expression.
- The ability to focus one's concentration on a single activity.
- A deep sensitivity to the pain of others.
- Mastery over a subject.
- Strong verbal skills that can make a point forcefully and positively, or can be used to cut others off at the knees.
- A sense of humor that keeps everything light.

When you talk about a skill no longer serving us, can you be more specific?

These skills may or may not be getting you what you want. A certain behavior may help you feel safe in the moment but also deprive you of something important. An example is my maintaining a distance from others. It might make me feel safe, but distance is not what I *really* want in all cases.

YOUR ACTION

It's time to take an inventory of the survival skills you developed over time. Ask yourself which ones you still use and how you use them. Ask yourself if you want to keep using them.

For the ones that are still valuable, are there any adjustments you would like to make?

Are you ready to drop the ones that no longer serve you? If so, do it in a non-judgmental way. In fact, *thank* these skills for helping you survive and tell them you appreciate them. Then let them know that they aren't helping anymore and release them.

This can be harder than it sounds. Look for your survival skills to be front and center when you feel unsafe. Start becoming conscious of when you are using ones that no longer serve you. Ask yourself what you could use as a replacement for that particular skill. Start developing skills more appropriate to your current life.

Here's an interesting thought. If you have identified skills that you would like to release and can't, ask yourself if this is because you actually still need them. If so, why do you still need them? Take a serious look at whether you have created danger in your life that requires the ongoing use of these skills. What are you going to do about that danger?

Chapter 23

LISTENING TO YOUR BODY

MY STORY

When I was a little girl and my father used to abuse me, he would sometimes tie me down with his neckties. Neckties were a smart choice, because they are wide and soft and don't leave distinct marks like a cord would. Mainly he tied down my arms.

Today, my hands and arms sometimes tighten unconsciously as if straining against some invisible restraint. It happens when I feel any situation threatening my freedom. The feeling is a warning signal that I don't feel safe.

This had been happening for years, even before the memories came. It used to freak me out. My arms seemed to have a life of their own. Over time, I have come to respect this response as evidence of my body's own unique way of warning me. It's a sign of the great intelligence of my body to interpret what is safe and what is not.

Over the years, I have come to respect my body's various ways of communicating with me. There is a place in my lower right back that sometimes spasms. When I was going through the most intense of my memory work, it would lock up for weeks at a time. Nothing could unlock it. The chiropractor didn't help for more than a few hours. Massages provided only temporary relief. Eventually it would go away. After this happened five or six times I started to notice a pattern. It would go away after I had released anger.

Now, when that place in my back starts to tighten up, I go within and ask what I am angry about. Usually I find the answer. Then I release it physically—through running or some other form of exertion. It's amazing—immediate relief. Boy, my body is really smart.

One of my friends frequently choked for no apparent reason. She's always had something going down the wrong pipe. She had been abused as a child and had always remembered the abuse, but never spoken of it. I believe her body was literally choking on the secret.

In incest survivor group I learned that it has been scientifically proven that trauma is stored at a cellular level. This being the case, our bodies can act as powerful instruments in our healing. They hold the abuse, giving us the opportunity to release it. Bodies are wise in a way our minds are not. If we can learn to listen to our bodies, they will help us heal.

OUR WALK

When you talk about listening to your body, how do you listen?

Eventually, awareness becomes natural to you. But, after years of being numb, you might not be able to be aware of your body at first. You may have to ask it what is going on.

That sounds pretty weird. How do you ask your body?

I talk to my body or I may write to it. I ask if there is something it's trying to tell me. I ask if there is something it is ready to release. Or if it knows what that particular pain or pressure is about. This sounds strange, I know, but I usually get an answer that allows me to move on.

What do you mean "an answer"? How does your body answer?

I usually find myself with what I can only describe as "knowing." Maybe not within that exact moment, but soon. I have found my body to be very wise. Sometimes it knows things my mind doesn't have a clue about.

What are other ways, besides talking or writing that you get in touch with your body?

Physical exercise, massage, yoga, meditation are good possibilities. There are many ways. Different ways work at different times. It's good to have a lot of tools from which to choose.

YOUR ACTION

Begin the practice of listening to your body. Honor whatever it is saying. Come to see it as your friend. Your guardian. It is there to protect you and to give you answers.

Ask yourself:

- Are there patterns of the location and type of pain I feel most often?
- Do I notice any relationship between what is happening around me and what I feel in my body?
- When I feel specific emotions, what do I feel in my body? (For example: fear = tightness in chest; anger = pain in lower back; shame = overall heaviness.)
- When I feel pain in my body, what was going on when the pain began?

Chapter 24

THRIVING

I want to share an aspect of my life that has supported my healing in a big way: the concepts I have learned in my career as a personal and business coach.

Being a coach is incredibly fulfilling to me. I specialize in helping entrepreneurs and small business owners optimize their lives and companies. When I began this career, I already was far along on the recovery journey. Yet the journey is so much more vivid and joyful because I have chosen this for my life's work.

The truth is, the coaching concepts in the next six chapters can enrich *anyone's* life. For an incest survivor, these concepts have special value in helping clear away clutter that can delay the healing process.

I was trained in these concepts at Coach U, founded by Thomas Leonard. Thousands of people besides myself are living more satisfying, joyful lives because of Thomas's work.

One of the first programs he created was called Personal Foundation, and the concepts I will share are drawn from it. I use them everyday—in my own life as well as with the clients I coach.

If you find these concepts as intriguing as I expect you will, here are resources for learning more:

- *The Portable Coach*, by Thomas Leonard, 1998, Scribner.
- Coach U (coachu.com)
- CoachVille (coachville.com)

If you are interested in working with a coach trained to guide people in the use of these concepts, refer to the list of Certified Graduates of Coach U on their website. You will also find a coach referral service on the website of the International Coach Federation (coachfederation.org).

Chapter 25

GETTING YOUR NEEDS MET

In the personal coaching field we often introduce clients to the idea of getting their needs met. This is a powerful skill that can be used to eliminate behaviors that are no longer serving us.

When I speak of getting your needs met, I'm referring to *personal* needs that are distinctive to you—not universal needs like food, water, air. A personal need is something that we feel driven to have, but for whatever reason we haven't been able to get *enough* of it to make that driven feeling go away.

I know my needs by heart. Safety is one. Peace is another. To be cared for is one more. And honesty is a fourth need of mine. Your own personal needs might be totally different. Maybe you crave acknowledgement. Or maybe you desire comfort in your life. There is no judgment attached. One's personal needs are what they are.

The point is that needs must be met in order for us to be happy. And what's really interesting is this—they <u>find</u> a way to *get met*. These needs drive our decisions, like the software that runs in the background of a computer drives what the machine does. But sometimes the way our personal needs get met is not in our best interest.

For an incest survivor, until you have entered the healing process, your deepest needs have gone unidentified and unmet. Even so, they have been working on you. Behind the scenes, these needs have been very busy, creating the patterns of behavior and thinking we so often find in our lives.

If you have a long-standing pattern of behavior that isn't serving you, but you haven't been able to break it, you can bet a need is the driving force behind it.

But how does a person figure out his or her personal needs? Thomas Leonard created the NeedLess Checklist for this purpose. It provides the means for determining what our top four needs are. Once we do this, we can figure out a way to get these priority needs met consciously.

Why is this so valuable? Because when we meet our needs consciously, they stop driving our decision-making behind the scenes, in ways that may not serve us well. I have found this understanding of personal needs to be one of the most effective tools I've ever encountered for breaking old, nonproductive patterns.

MY STORY

Running was an important part of my healing. It helped me process emotions. It gave me a sense of strength and accomplishment. And those endorphins! What a great way to feel great.

For many years I had a running partner. We trained together several times a week and ran all over Atlanta on our long runs. When she decided to move outside the city it became logistically impractical to run together on a regular basis, so I began running alone. I noticed a big change in the quality of my runs. A tension developed around my running that had not been there before. The joy went out of running, so much so that I almost decided to give it up.

My personal need for safety was not being met—this was the problem. With a partner, I had always felt safe running in the city. Without one, I was feeling vulnerable. What I didn't know then, that I know now, was that my need for safety was so strong that it was interfering with my ability to lead my life the way I wanted.

Fortunately, the idea came to me to buy a Rottweiler, one of those big black and brown dogs that would give pause to any sane person who might want to harm me. Bear, who has become a beloved pet, has met my need for safety all the years since. My running became fun again. Understanding the personal need that was driving my decision-making, and figuring out how to meet it, prevented that need from causing me to give up something that was very beneficial.

OUR WALK

So how was it that you managed to get that safety need met before you even knew about "needs"?

Luck. Instinct. It just worked out that way. What's really cool is that with Thomas Leonard's NeedLess Checklist, we no longer have to be hit or miss about it. We can consciously determine our needs and meet them in a way that serves us.

Let me refer you to the needs discussion in his book *The Portable Coach*, p. 161. (Step 13: Getting Your Personal Needs Met, Once and For All)

The way I apply it is to take the following steps:

- Identify your top four needs (see the Your Action section that follows)

- Set up a way to get each of these needs met in a conscious way that is automatic, ongoing and healthy.

What do you mean by "conscious, automatic, ongoing and healthy"?

- <u>Automatic</u> – happens without you having to take any special action that isn't a natural part of your life.
- <u>Conscious</u> – something you do intentionally, with forethought.
- <u>Ongoing</u> – you plan for it to continue indefinitely.
- <u>Healthy</u> – it serves you well.

Bear, my Rottweiler, is a great example of all these attributes. Buying this dog was a *conscious* decision to deter anyone who might harm me. She lives here now—it's *automatic*. I don't have to do anything special to protect myself—she goes out the front door with me every time I go out. She's an *ongoing* protection—as long as she lives, she will protect me. She is a *healthy* way to meet my need for safety, as opposed to the option of giving up running.

If I do this, get my needs met, what can I expect to happen?

Lots! You may notice that you are less dependent on others or on external circumstances for your happiness. You may see long-standing patterns of dysfunctional behavior between yourself and others start to disappear. You may find yourself making very different decisions than would have been true in the past. In short, your life will start working better.

This is powerful stuff. Give it a try!

Why is it especially important for incest survivors to learn to get their needs met?

As children, many of our basic needs were ignored. So, more than some people, we never developed the skills to even know what our needs are, much less get them met. That's why learning about how to understand and take responsibility for our own needs is so empowering for incest survivors.

YOUR ACTION

Take the NeedLess Checklist. Go on the internet and do a search for the NeedLess Program. One of the top search results will be a pdf file you can download and print out.

Read everything in the Checklist through Step Two, *but* I would suggest you follow a slightly different assessment procedure than in the instructions. Here's what I want you to do:

- Highlight all the words that you believe are needs for you.
- Go back and count how many words you have highlighted in each category.
- Write down the names of the categories that have the top four most words highlighted or circled. These are your top four needs. If you have a tie, go with your "gut" as to which is a higher need for you.

List your top four needs below:

Need #1 _____

Need #2 _____

Need #3 _____

Need #4 _____

Simply identifying your needs is a powerful step. Knowing what they are increases your awareness about who *you* are.

As you consider your top four needs, ask yourself these questions:

- In what ways are these needs getting themselves met today?
- Are those ways serving me well?
- Do I see these needs behind patterns in my life?
- Are there better ways to get these needs met than the ways I am using?

- As I reflect on times I have been very upset with a person or situation, can I see how the root cause was that one or more of my needs was not being met?

Okay, so you know what your needs are and have a basic understanding that they have been driving your decision-making. Now what?

Now it's time to get them met *consciously,* in an *automatic, ongoing and healthy* way.

Take one need at a time and consider what *system* you can install in your life to meet that need. What do we mean by a *system*? Something that, once in place, works in an automatic and ongoing way. My Rottweiler is a system.

Here's another example. After I had sold my former business and gone to Coach U, I decided to become a full-time coach. In making the transition, I accepted a job running a company in Louisville, Kentucky for a year. That meant flying each week to Louisville and back.

As I considered whether to accept the job, I felt conflicted. On one hand, I could do it in three days a week so it left lots of time to build my coaching practice. And the job paid well. I felt torn, however. By then, I had studied needs in my coach training. I realized that one of my needs was generating the conflicted feelings. It was my need to feel cared for!

Flying to Louisville and back each week felt like a lot of wear and tear— getting to the airport, dealing with parking hassles, lugging my stuff, lots of waiting. I knew I wouldn't feel cared for if I did that for the entire year. So, I decided to make a request of my husband. I asked him if he would be willing to take me to the airport and pick me up every week for a year. Big request! He gave it a lot of thought and decided that was something he was willing to do. (Have I mentioned he's the greatest guy on the planet?)

What happened? Well, it was great! Instead of feeling like a worn-out road warrior, I really enjoyed our time together riding to and from to the airport. Each time I returned, Paul picked me up and took me out to dinner and we discussed our time apart. Very romantic. I felt wrapped in the perpetual warmth of feeling cared for.

This is a great example of how a conscious understanding of the way our needs work can make an enormous difference in quality of life. Without that awareness, I would have taken the job because that was what made the most sense to do. But I would have felt conflicted and not been sure why. I would have resented the travel. I would have been hard to live with. There would have been conflict. You get the picture. Instead, I had a whole year of getting my need to feel cared for met. What a difference!

113

That's a *system*. Paul taking me to the airport and picking me up was a system that met my need to feel cared for.

Your action is to install, over time, a system for meeting each one of your top four needs. You may find that one system can satisfy more than one need. If so, great!

Here are a couple of pointers. You can get your needs met in a variety of ways:

- Meet them yourself.
- Make a request of another.
- Buy something – a thing or a service.
- Trade something – a thing or a service – with someone.

Anytime you find yourself very upset about something, ask what need is not being met. Then, ask yourself how you will get it met in a conscious, automatic, ongoing and healthy way.

This work is very powerful and takes place over time. You may find it helpful to work with a professional coach trained to help in the identification and understanding of needs. (Go to the coach referral service at coachu.com.)

Chapter 26

SETTING BOUNDARIES

Earlier in the book I referred to boundaries, which are conditions we put in place in our lives that help us become clear about what we will and will not accept from others. This is a topic worth exploring more deeply.

Our boundaries help us define where *we* end and the rest of the world begins. Because incest survivors were not allowed to have their own protected internal space as children, this concept is important for us. Our boundaries have been violated enormously. Setting them now is a powerful way to reclaim our very selves.

MY STORY

I had a good friend who was a recovering alcoholic when we met. She hadn't had a drink in nine years. We grew close over time. I enjoyed her company and we shared some very special times together. After I had known her for five years, she began to drink again. Hers was a typical attitude, "Just one, I can handle it." It wasn't long until she had fallen back into the destructive lifestyle of a raging alcoholic.

By the time of her relapse, I had done a lot of work with boundaries. One of the boundaries I had set for myself was that I would not allow drunks in my life. My father had been a drunk, and I simply wasn't going to deal with that type of destructive energy again.

I had a very hard decision to make. It was clear my friend was not going to give up drinking again any time soon, if ever. Would I enforce the boundary and risk losing her as a friend, or would I compromise the boundary and tolerate something I said I would not?

When she was in a sober moment, I went to her and told her that I loved her. I expressed concern that her drinking was very destructive to her life and that if she ever wanted my support to stop drinking, I would do anything I could. Then I told her about my boundary. Her choices were totally up to her and I wasn't trying to change her, but as long as she continued to drink, she couldn't be in my life.

This happened almost ten years ago. I haven't seen her since. I still love her and she's welcome back in my life at any time she is willing to commit to sobriety.

Boundaries can be hard to keep. Sometimes we have to give up cherished things in order to preserve what we honor even more—ourselves.

OUR WALK

If you weren't raised with good boundaries, how do you even start setting them?

Look at the needs you have articulated. Then write boundaries that will help get each of your needs met. Formalize them; don't just leave them in your head.

For example, I have a need for safety. Here are some of my boundaries related to safety:

- No one is allowed to raise his/her voice to me.
- No one may touch me without my permission.
- Abusive people may have no role in my personal or professional life.
- Active alcoholics cannot be in my life.

How does simply writing a boundary change the actions of others?

Once you establish a boundary, you do need to communicate it. This is usually harder with people you already know, because you will be changing the ground rules they are used to. It's best to first communicate your boundaries at a time that is not emotionally intense—when the other person is more likely to hear you.

One approach: Find a time when it feels comfortable to simply say that you have been looking at what you need to have in place to live the kind of life you want. As a result, you have decided to establish some boundaries. You would like to let him/her know what these boundaries are and ask that they be respected.

What happens if a boundary is not respected?

Then you restate it to the person who attempted to cross it. You may also need to impose a consequence if restating it doesn't work. For example, if my boundary that no one is allowed to raise his/her voice to me is being violated, then I might do the following:

First, restate. "You know, John, I have requested that you not raise your voice to me."

Then, if John continues to raise his voice, "John, it is not acceptable to me that you are yelling at me. Please stop or we will have to discontinue our discussion."

If he continues, I would leave the situation by saying "I will not continue this discussion while you are yelling at me. I would be happy to discuss the matter when you are able to speak respectfully to me."

I can imagine that setting boundaries could make the people around you pretty mad. What do you do about that?

You're right. It can be very upsetting to the balance of relationships. People who are intimidating, controlling or manipulative usually have a pretty strong reaction when you set boundaries with them.

Remember, they are *your* boundaries. No one else gets a vote! Don't debate whether they are fair. That is for you alone to decide. Also remember that your boundaries are about *you*, and no one else. If the other person has a reaction, *that's* about them. Let them have their reaction and deal with it—it's not your job. Just keep communicating the boundary. If unfortunately, you see over time that someone is unwilling to respect your boundaries, you may decide that person can't have a prominent place in your life.

It's *your* choice to have the boundary. It's *their* choice to respect it or not.

This boundary thing seems like a lot of work. I mean, do you go around giving everyone you meet a list of your boundaries?

It's interesting—once you have *internalized* a boundary (meaning you have really made it a part of your life), people rarely violate it. It's as if they know the boundary is there without you even having to say it.

I work with a lot of business owners and high-level corporate executives. Some are big bullies used to treating those around them less than respectfully. It's funny, but they are *always* respectful to me. *Always*. It's because of my boundaries. They just know I'm not one to be disrespected.

Why is it particularly powerful for an incest survivor to set and maintain strong boundaries?

Most incest survivors lack boundaries because, when they were young, what should have been their boundaries were totally ignored. So they never learned the skill of setting boundaries and having them honored. A child is too small to enforce what he or she intuitively knows is right, never developing that sense of "this is where I end and the world begins."

As adults, we can reclaim our territory—ourselves. Setting boundaries is a powerful step in that direction.

YOUR ACTION

Write a list of boundaries for yourself.

Start by looking at your needs and asking what boundaries you want to put in place to help your needs get met. You could also start with areas of your life that aren't working well and ask if boundaries would help.

Communicate your boundaries to those who need to hear them.

Enforce your boundaries with consequences, if necessary.

Chapter 27

RAISING YOUR STANDARDS

If boundaries are our requirements for the behavior of others toward us, standards are our requirements for our own behavior.

What do we expect of ourselves? How will we conduct ourselves in the world?

Standards help define a sense of who we are and what we stand for. Raising our standards helps us feel good about ourselves. It also helps our lives work better.

MY STORY

As I healed and started rebuilding my foundation, I started changing. I got my act together. I began feeling better about myself. I started evaluating what was working in my life and what wasn't.

But, something wasn't right. I came to realize that my physical environment was the problem. It didn't fit with my internal self anymore. Inside, I was feeling clean and clear. Outside, my office and house were cluttered.

I raised my standard. This became my new standard:

My external environment will support a sense of peace and clarity.

This required making big changes. I threw out clutter and made room. I organized. I beautified. What a huge difference! My energy shifted due to my external surroundings.

If you want to elevate your quality of life, raising your standards is a great first step.

OUR WALK

Could you give a few examples of standards?

Sure. But, please remember, these will be different for everyone. You have to decide what *your* standards are.

- I am on time for all client appointments.
- I exercise regularly.
- I eat a diet that is healthy for me.
- I only stay in environments that are safe.
- I keep a reserve of money that enables me to choose which clients I accept.
- I have the support services I need to allow me to do only the things I love to do.

How does having high standards fit in with healing from incest?

I believe there is a definite link. Our self-image was damaged by the abuse we endured. We got the message that we were not worth respecting, therefore not deserving of having high standards. Setting and maintaining standards can go a long way toward helping restore our self-respect.

YOUR ACTION

Ask yourself:

- What's working and what's not working in my life?
- What is something I still do that is no longer consistent with whom I am?
- In what areas could my life use an upgrade?
- What is one thing I could do that would make me feel dramatically better about myself?

Write your standards.

Here's an important note. Make sure your standards are something you really *want*. Don't make them a "should" or an "ought". Don't make them what somebody else's standards are. If you don't really want them, you won't uphold them and you'll feel bad about yourself as a result. That's not the goal we want here. We want standards that help us feel great about who we are. Never, ever use standards as a way to beat yourself up.

Chapter 28

STOP TOLERATING!

Another concept Thomas Leonard introduced to me was the concept of what he called "tolerations." Tolerations are those things in our lives that we are putting up with. They can be small, like a cluttered drawer or big, like living in a home you don't like.

We become numb to our tolerations. We don't even notice them. But they drain our energy each and every day. Friction comes into our lives because of them, distracting us from what is important.

MY STORY

Several years ago, I bought a small sailboat. It seemed like a good idea at the time but I found that I rarely used it—probably less than once a year. It sat in the driveway and blocked the way when we needed to move something large into the backyard. It gathered leaves and filled with water. In short, it became a toleration.

Every time I pulled into the driveway, I noticed it. Sitting there. Not being used. Gathering debris. It drained my energy.

Last week, I gave it to a local children's charity for their camp. Whew! What a relief. Just to see an uncluttered driveway. To no longer have the thought "I really need to get rid of that thing" every time I saw it.

It's amazing how much energy eliminating a toleration can free up.

OUR WALK

Can you give other examples of stopping tolerations?

There are many degrees of tolerations. Here are some simple ones I have eliminated over the years:

- Not having a place to consistently put my car keys
- Having to do my own financial bookkeeping

121

- A leaky faucet
- A window that wouldn't roll down in the car
- Not enough light in my office closet
- File drawers that kept getting stuck

Here are some more challenging tolerations I have tackled and eliminated:

- A client who was always late for our sessions
- A porch I could only use 6 or 7 months a year
- A friend who had a habit of criticizing me
- Neighbors who were loud late at night
- Allergies

I feel overwhelmed when you talk about tolerations. Do I have to handle them all at once?

Absolutely not. In fact, I suggest you only handle things when it feels like the right time. Start with something simple, something you can handle in less than five minutes, like hanging up a hook for your car keys. See how you feel afterward. Usually, you will feel good—more energetic. Change that burned out light bulb in the closet, and you will feel good every time you walk in there.

I'm not making the connection between tolerations and incest recovery. Why are tolerations important for an incest survivor to deal with?

Tolerations are an issue for everyone, but they have special significance for a person who had to tolerate so much as a child. As incest survivors, we became pretty numb as we had to accept what was imposed on us. In adulthood, we usually continue those patterns.

Tolerating something sends a subtle message to ourselves that we aren't worthy of having a truly great life, free of things that bring us down. Eliminating tolerations is an exercise of power, helping us feel better about our lives and ourselves. It also frees up our energy so we can focus on our healing. In fact, I believe many incest survivors fill their lives with tolerations so they won't have the time or energy to really look at what is scaring them within.

YOUR ACTION

Make a list of 50 things you are tolerating. Make it without committing to do anything about them. Just make the list.

If you can't think of 50, keep digging. You may be numb to all you are tolerating. Part of this process is to become *aware*.

When you have finished, you may decide to start eliminating only small tolerations. Or, you may feel motivated to start big.

If you want to start small, pick something that would be easy to eliminate and do it. Right now! Do something small each day for a week. Work up to the bigger things.

If you want to start big, here's something to think about. Within our list of tolerations there are often what Thomas Leonard calls lynchpin tolerations. Those are the ones that, if we eliminate them, a number of other tolerations go away with them. An example would be that by changing jobs you might eliminate the tolerations of an abusive boss, work you don't like, a long commute and not making enough money. All at the same time!

Ask yourself what your lynchpin tolerations are. Don't tackle them until you are ready. When you decide you are ready, eliminating lynchpin tolerations will greatly accelerate your progress.

I am aware that some of my examples of getting rid of tolerations may sound over the top to some people. Most people aren't ready to march off and do these things just from reading a book. The point of including them is to emphasize that if you steadily practice eliminating tolerations, you may work up to some very significant changes in your life.

Ultimately, the goal is to eliminate all the tolerations from your life. I know that sounds ambitious, but once you start, it feels so good that you are likely to keep going. And once you are living a toleration-free life, you will be careful to avoid adding new tolerations. You will eliminate them before they ever take hold.

Chapter 29

GETTING COMPLETE

Another concept from my coach training that I think can be immensely helpful to incest survivors is called "incompletions." Very much like tolerations, incompletions drain our energy and take our focus off what is most important.

Incompletions are things or situations that feel unfinished in a way that nags at us. A conversation we had that just didn't feel right. The project we started six months ago and is still sitting on the dining table.

Just as with tolerations, we easily become numb to incompletions. Gaining awareness of them and "getting complete" can help you use your energy more effectively and allow you to focus on more productive aspects of your life.

MY STORY

Early in my coach training, I interviewed four coaches to be my mentor coach. I liked them all and knew I would have a hard time deciding which one I wanted to work with. I told each one that I would let him or her know what I was going to do after I finished interviewing all four. I decided which coach I wanted to work with and set up a time to get started. I wrote on my to-do list, "Let coaches know I will be working with another coach."

Somehow I always found something else on that list to do instead. The item stayed on my to-do list, but I never called the other three coaches. I felt badly about not doing what I had said I would do. A year went by.

I started studying incompletions and realized that this was a big one for me. I hadn't been aware of how much it had drained me. There it was, first thing every morning, on my list. I realized it was taking a lot of energy to avoid it.

I decided to get complete with the three coaches. It took less than 15 minutes to make those calls. Fifteen minutes to eliminate a weight I had carried for over a year! I felt as if I had just taken the weight of the world off my shoulders—and the interesting thing was that I hadn't even been conscious of carrying it.

OUR WALK

What should I look for to identify incompletions?

See if any of these ring a bell:

- Questions about your financial status
- Remaining undecided about whether to accept an invitation
- Unfinished "thank you" notes
- Holiday decorations that are still in boxes under the stairs in the living room
- Those 15 unfinished books sitting on your nightstand
- That nagging feeling that Mary sounded angry with you in your last conversation
- The uncomfortable conversation you know you need to have with your boss

Are unrecovered memories incompletions?

I believe so ... but I am not recommending that you try to force them into your consciousness. As we have discussed, memories come when you are ready to have them.

What about confronting the abuser or telling about the incest? Are those incompletions?

They are only incompletions at the point that you *know* you are ready to do them.

You may very legitimately decide that it would never be good—for the rest of your life—to confront your abuser. Once you make peace with this decision, there is no incompletion involved. It's only an incompletion if you feel the need to do something and not doing it is costing you.

YOUR ACTION

First, list all the incompletions you can think of.
Next, pick one to complete. You may want to start small.

Also, as with tolerations, there may be lynchpin incompletions. (This is an incompletion, which when complete, completes several others all at once.) If you want to make a big move, pick one of those.

Keep getting complete with things—at your own pace. Again, a professional coach can be very helpful with this work.

Chapter 30

LIVING YOUR VALUES

In coaching, I often tell my clients to orient their lives around their values. What I am referring to are not the traditional ethical values. Rather, I'm talking about the values we all have that are the truest expression of who we are.

When you are living your life in a way that expresses your values, you are living a very satisfying life. You are probably coming pretty close to touching the reason you are on this planet. That's a big statement, and it's true.

An important connection exists between needs, which I discussed earlier, and values. When needs remain unconscious and drive our decision-making without our acknowledging them, it's hard to focus on our values. So we live in a way that is "out of phase" with the essence of who we are. Once we get our needs met consciously, we are then free to make decisions that allow us to live a life that expresses our values.

MY STORY

I began to dread getting up in the mornings. I despised starting another day because it meant going to work. I hated my job—even though I owned the company. What was that about?

It was about feeling unfulfilled. I had, in a matter of years, been a finalist for two prestigious business awards. I owned one of the most respected companies of our kind in the country. Yet, I didn't get much satisfaction from it.

What I know now, that I didn't know then, is that I wasn't living my values. (My needs weren't getting met either, which certainly compounded things.)

As I learned about coaching, I did a lot of values clarification and realized my most important values were To Catalyze, To Create, Freedom, and Mastery. These values had been expressed in my work in the first years of the business when I was building the company. Now that it was up and running, these same values weren't being honored.

When I sold the business, I felt as if I had my freedom back. That's when I went to coaching school and started a new career. I've been able to construct a life that expresses my values each day in everything I do. This is the ultimate!

OUR WALK

I'm still not clear about values in the way you use the term.

Your values are the essence of who you are. Look at what you chose to do when you were six years old—the games you liked, your favorite stories. Chances are you were expressing your values. Even now, when you are engaged in an activity that expresses one of your values, it feels like time disappears. You look up and six hours have passed, and you have forgotten to eat. That's when you are living a value.

Why are values something that's important for an incest survivor to understand?

We have been taught not to set the bar of expectations very high. Early on, we learned that life is tough and we can't have it our way. But … we *can*! That's the whole message of this book. By understanding what is fulfilling to us and acting upon it as described in these pages, we *can* have life our way.

Selling your business to honor your values is a pretty drastic step. Do you really think people who are in the ravages of incest recovery will be able to make such dramatic moves?

This is a very important question. It's all about timing and not forcing things before you are ready for them. In this book, I have laid out a progression of healing practices. While the progress is not completely linear, it is unlikely that someone will be ready to tackle needs and values before she/he has tackled creating a safe space. One of the most important messages in this book is for each reader to take on new concepts when he/she is ready. Each person will move back and forth among these concepts, as her/his healing requires.

YOUR ACTION

Use the Tru Values Program. Go on the internet and search for "tru values". One of the top responses will be a pdf file to download and print out.

Read from the beginning through Step Two. As with the NeedLess Program, I'd like to change the instructions a bit. Here's what to do:

- Go through the list of words and highlight the ones you believe are your values.
- Write the number you have highlighted in each category by the category title.
- Divide that number by the total number of words in that category to get a percentage. (If there were ten words and you highlighted six of them, your percentage for that category is 60%)
- Find the four categories with the highest percentages.
- Write them below.

My top four values:

#1 _____

#2 _____

#3 _____

#4 _____

Now, ask yourself the following questions:

- Are these values (my essence) being expressed in the way I live and work?
- What is my level of satisfaction with my life, and how might that relate to my values?
- What action could I take to make my values a natural part of how I live?

Chapter 31

STAYING PRESENT

Most incest survivors have mastered the art of going away, mentally and emotionally. When things occurred in the past that were beyond our ability to deal with, we learned how to simply *not be there,* even when our bodies were. It was a survival skill. It helped us not go crazy. It was necessary.

Now it's not. Now it causes us to miss out on the present moment. And the present moment is the *only* place life can be lived. The end result is that we actually miss out on a lot of our life that could be very fulfilling.

We need to learn a new skill. It's called "staying present."

MY STORY

There was a woman in my incest group who would simply go away when a topic hit too close to home for her. She remained physically in the room, but she was no longer with us. The first few times it happened, I didn't even notice. The therapists did, however, and they would use techniques to bring her back. I thought this was a really weird thing for her to do. Then I realized I did the same thing on a regular basis. The only difference was that I did a better job of covering it up. People never even knew when I wasn't there. And here's the real kicker: *I* never even noticed when I wasn't there.

This was an issue.

Then one day I picked up a book because I loved the title. It was *Wherever You Go, There You Are: Mindfulness Meditation in Everyday Life* by Jon Kabat-Zinn. This book introduced me to the concept of staying present. I came to realize that in our distraction-filled world, this is an issue for all humans, not just incest survivors. But I believe survivors of abuse have especially big challenges staying present.

As I came to understand the concept, I realized that I was *hardly ever* present. To me, this connected directly with the fact that I didn't feel much joy in my life. When you aren't *in* your life, you can't experience what's going on. I came to understand that being present with what's going on, whatever it is, is a joyful experience. We can only live in the present moment. Miss out on the present and you miss out on your life. That means missing out on the joy of being alive.

With time and effort, I have cultivated my ability to stay present. There are lots of ways to do this. I will discuss my personal choice—meditation. You can find books, classes and other resources that deeply explore this subject. My comments are just a starting point.

I often use a form of meditation in which you simply sit still and pay attention to your breath. This sounds simple, and it is. Yet it is also very challenging because of the tendency of our mind to wander. I start by counting my breaths, one through ten, then start back at one again. The first several weeks I tried this I rarely got to ten. It was hard to stay focused on even this simple task. Suddenly I would realize that my mind had been elsewhere for five or ten minutes and I had stopped counting and never even noticed. It was amazing.

Eventually I was able to stay present for longer periods of time. You may be asking "So what?" The "so what" is that when you cultivate your ability to stay present while meditating, you *also* cultivate your ability to stay present in life! This creates a sense of wonderment.

Words cannot adequately express the delight of simply *being here*. The joy of feeling it all and being with it all, no matter what is happening. Learning to stay present means learning to reclaim your life to the fullest extent. I highly recommend it.

OUR WALK

So all you did is count your breaths and you learned to stay present?

The meditation was a big part of it. It's the practice that leads to the ability to stay present. You can't just study about meditation, you have to *do* it. Along with the actual practice of meditation, I read numerous books on Buddhism and listened to talks by teachers. I learned a form of meditation called Insight Meditation from an excellent set of audiotapes by Sharon Salzberg and Joseph Goldstein. It's called *Insight Meditation—An In-Depth Correspondence Course.* Another very in-depth audio series is *The Science of Enlightenment* by Shinzen Young. There are also hundreds of meditation centers where you can learn to meditate.

I can't just sit like that. It would drive me nuts!

There are many ways to mediate. There is a form of meditation called walking meditation. Many books on the subject describe how to do it. Again, it's very simple. If you find it hard to sit still, try walking meditation.

Do you mean you have to constantly fight your mind to stay present?

No. This is not about fighting. It's the opposite. It's about observing and accepting. It's about noticing that you have drifted away, and then gently coming back.

What about when things are too intense to stay present?

Then don't try to do so. As you cultivate your ability to stay present, you will naturally be able to do so at higher level of intensity. The important thing is simply to notice when you have gone away and bring yourself back to the present. And it's also very important not to *judge* yourself for this. Don't use the practice of staying present to beat yourself up. Just notice when you have gone away and bring yourself back to the present. Eventually, you will stay present more often and through more intense experiences.

Are you talking about staying present in the present, or are you talking about staying present with your feelings as they come up about the past?

Both, because they each are occurring in the present. Staying present in the present takes place now. So does staying present with your feelings as they come up about the past. They are coming up in the present. Be with them, don't run from them. Stay with them now, because it's safe to do so now. The incest isn't happening *now*. These feelings are left over from *then*, but they are absolutely with you now. Now is your opportunity to be with them and let them go—something you couldn't do, mentally and emotionally, when you were being abused because you had to go away to survive.

YOUR ACTION

Try this as an introduction to meditating. Sit cross-legged on the floor on a pillow so that your bottom is higher than your legs or sit on a chair with your feet on the floor. Put your hands on your thighs or place them in your lap with one hand cupping the other. Either close your eyes or let your gaze fall down at about a 45-degree angle. Start by taking slow deep breaths into your belly. Notice each breath. Turn your breathing over to your body. Don't force it. Continue to notice the breath. Count each breath, in and out. Count up to ten and begin again.

Try doing this for five minutes. Notice how present you are able to stay. Do this daily. When you are able to stay present for five minutes, gradually increase the time.

Bring this quality of "mindfulness" that you are cultivating to everything you do in your life. Stay present with things. Notice when you have gone away. Bring yourself back. Do it over and over again.

Notice how this changes the quality of your life experience.

Chapter 32

BEYOND "SURVIVOR"

I love the quote in the front of this book from Eckhart Tolle.
"The truth is that the only power there is, is contained within this moment: it is the power of your presence. Once you know that, you also realize that *you* are responsible for your inner space now—nobody else is—and that the past cannot prevail against the power of the Now."

To someone who has been abused, this means there is something beyond that identity. We must no longer believe that the past is more powerful than the present.

MY STORY

So, I learned early in my healing process to call myself a "survivor" rather than a "victim." It was very helpful, because the word "victim" felt like I was still trapped in the abuse. The word "survivor" meant I had broken loose and made it through.

At first, when I claimed the truth of my childhood, it was such a relief. I finally understood parts of myself that had been a mystery to me. I had a *reason* for being who I was and acting as I acted. I finally knew why I was so different.

This must be how people feel who have suffered for years from mysterious medical symptoms and then finally are given a diagnosis. "Oh, so I've been tired for years because I am diabetic. Now I understand." It legitimizes how you have been feeling and acting.

As I started telling my story, as the words flowed more and more smoothly, "survivor" became a badge of honor. A source of pride. I became identified with that word. It became my story. For a long, long time, that identity was very useful. In fact, my hope is that all incest survivors come so fully to live the survivor identity that they burn out all the shame and guilt in the process. It gives definition and voice to all that which once was hidden and buried and eating us alive. Claiming the survivor identity forces the secret into the light of day, where like all things that thrive in darkness, it shrinks and loses power.

I was a Survivor with a capital "S," a professional survivor. I learned to hide behind it, to wear it as armor, to use it to my advantage. I could tell my story and have immediate respect. My identity as an incest survivor became my new interface with the world.

Truth to tell, I didn't want to give it up. It was the first self-shaped identity I had ever really had, and I liked it. Behind that identity, I was safe. And, after years of embracing it, I knew I had to grow beyond it. This was a big turning point in my healing process. As I look back on it, I realize it showed how much I had healed.

OUR WALK

How did you know you needed to grow beyond identifying yourself as a survivor?

When I used that identity to allow me to stop growing. When I told myself I couldn't do something that scared me because I'm an incest survivor and I just couldn't do that. When I used it to get people's respect—for the fact I survived —not for who I really am today. When I really needed to ask the question, "Who am I beyond being a survivor?"

Does this mean, in any way, that you have grown ashamed of being a survivor?

No! Absolutely not! I will always be a survivor and be proud of that part of me. But, I am a lot of other things. I want to claim all the parts of me. I don't want to be limited to being only a survivor.

Do you have a new word you use now?

Not really, beyond my name. I'm at a stage when I'd rather not try to define myself with just one word. I am part of the constant ebb and flow of energy that moves through the universe and creates our world. That's a little hard to put into one word.

YOUR ACTION

What I suggest now is only for when you are ready, okay? Only after you have moved from Victim to Survivor and fully embraced being a Survivor.

Make a list of all your attributes. See how broad you can go. That's all. Just become aware of all that you are.

Then, the next time you meet someone that you might be willing to share your survivor story with, refrain from doing so. See what happens. See how you introduce yourself to the world without that being your whole story.

Chapter 33

LEGACY

We've talked about how to move from victim to survivor. And about expanding your identity beyond survivor. But what's beyond that? I believe the ultimate purpose of our lives—and the final stage of our healing process—is to give back. To leave a legacy.

A person's legacy is intricately connected to his or her purpose in life. And I believe that this purpose reveals itself over time.

You don't go in search of it. It finds you. When it does, you know it. And when you know it—what your own purpose is—you begin to understand what your legacy might be.

At this point, life gets incredibly interesting. This is what makes it all—the good and bad, the pain and joy, everything—worthwhile.

MY STORY

For years my life was filled with contaminated relationships. They epitomized the term "co-dependent". I would find people whose lives weren't working and try to "save" them. Share my wisdom with them. Give them endless support. Give until there was no more to give. It was awful. A dead-end. I finally "got it" that I had better save myself first!

Once I learned that "saving" others was just a way to avoid doing my own hard work, I pretty much gave it up. In fact, I went to the other extreme. I wasn't going to be a savior to anyone. For a time it became very important to me that I not be one of those people out there trying to save the world. I had been at such an extreme on the "saving" continuum that I had to move to the other end for a while before it could balance out.

After several years at the opposite end of the spectrum, I had to ask myself, "So is all the suffering you went through just your own private tragedy? Did it serve no other purpose than to make you strong and cunning? Did it produce no greater good than teaching you survivor skills and giving you a vehicle for self awareness?" Something told me I was finally ready to give back.

Thus, this book, and my career as a professional business coach.

I stepped slowly into this "giving back" thing. It scared me because I had done it for the wrong reasons for so long. In the past, I had given as a way to be needed, to feel powerful, to deserve love.

My old way of giving sent the message to others "Let me do it for you, since you don't have it within you to do it yourself." This was harmful. It took their power away.

I needed to learn some important things before I could give back in a positive way. Before I could leave a legacy.

First, I came to the belief that all of us have the capacity to learn and change. While I may be the catalyst for such learning and changing, everyone holds the power to make such shifts for themselves.

So, when others try to give me the credit for their life being better, I don't accept it. *They* did it. Not me. I cannot change anyone. I may share some insights that another internalizes and works with, but make no mistake, each individual does the work for him or herself.

Next, I had to learn to detach from the outcome. If you are "helping" another and are attached to the outcome of a situation, then it's really not about helping the other person, it's about you. When you can detach from the outcome, then you are pretty "clean" in your giving. The term "no strings attached" becomes authentic.

Finally, the most important thing I learned about legacy is that it comes through me, but not from me. That may sound odd, but it's true.

When I am in a state of true giving, I know that what's being given flows from some higher source through me. It's effortless. This understanding has changed my whole perspective on giving. The time was when giving used to tire me. I couldn't give too much, or I felt I would run out. As I learned to let the giving flow through me, I realized that there is an endless supply. It no longer tires me.

This is it! This is sheer *joy*. To come full circle, tapping into a higher, transformative power. To take a localized event that happened to me as an individual and use it as a force for healing on our planet.

We all can do this. *You* can do this. At some point, you can take your pain and transform it into a powerful force for good in this world. It won't be in the same way I have done it. It will be your way. And your way will find you when you are ready. Your only job is to make yourself ready. Do that by healing.

OUR WALK

What do you mean by saying that you were trying to help others in the wrong way?

I came to realize that what I was doing wasn't about helping at all. It was about me, my way to avoid doing my own work. If I could focus on others, I didn't have to be with me. If they could absorb my time and energy, I didn't have to face my own demons. And if I could get them to depend on me, then maybe they wouldn't abandon me. They might even give me something that felt like love. But I learned that working with others when I had this kind of mindset wasn't helping, it was hurting.

It seems like when you say you detach from the outcome that you don't care about what happens to the other person. Is that what you really mean?

I care deeply. And yet, I can let go. I care *and* detach at the same time. It empowers the other person to take my gift and do with it what he/she will. Without my judging or wanting it to turn out a certain way. I think it's one of the most respectful things we can do for each other. Care *and* detach.

You lost me when you said giving comes through you, but not from you. Can you tell me more about this?

Let's take writing this book as an example. It has been effortless. I sit down with my laptop and see if something comes. If it does, I start writing it down. It flows. It comes through my heart much more than through my head. And I am absolutely certain that it comes from a place beyond my own limited self. It comes from a universal consciousness. Some would call it God or a higher power. I believe that each of us is here to connect with this "flow." I believe that by connecting with this higher power and becoming a conduit of wisdom into the world, we are living our life purpose. We are leaving our legacy.

I always get confused when I think about big concepts like "What is my purpose in life?" How do you go about discovering that?

As I said, it's really more about it finding you than you finding it. A book I found particularly insightful is Dawna Markova's *I Will Not Die an Unlived Life: Reclaiming Purpose and Passion.* It's a nice roadmap.

YOUR ACTION

Your actions here will depend on where you are in your healing process.

If you are just beginning your healing process ...
Don't focus on legacy just yet. Just know that you will eventually leave a legacy. Focus, for now, on yourself.

If you are in the middle of your healing process ...
Take a hard look at the ways in which you are "giving" and ask yourself these questions:

- Do I get a charge out of giving?
- Do I become angry, hurt or frustrated when people don't appreciate all I do for them?
- Do I give more in my relationships than I get back?

If the answer is "yes" to any of these questions, then stop trying to give for a while. I know that sounds selfish, but you will really be doing everyone a favor, including yourself.

Instead of focusing on others, ask yourself:

- What have I been giving to others that I really need to be giving to myself?
- What can I do to show myself the love I seek from others?
- What need am I satisfying by giving to others that I really need to meet myself?

If you are through the bulk of your healing work ...
Become still. Focus on "being" rather than "doing." Get quiet enough to hear the call. Open your mind to the endless possibilities for your life. Connect to pursuits that you feel passion for. Give it as much time as it needs. Your purpose will find you. And you will know it when it does. Trust that this will happen.

While you are waiting, grow yourself. Read books to expand your horizons. Associate with people who seem to come from a place of higher consciousness. When you are ready, your purpose will be clear. That's when you will know what your legacy is.

AFTERWORD

I want to circle back to Eckhart Tolle's words quoted at the beginning of this book.

A victim identity is the belief that the past is more powerful than the present, which is the opposite of the truth.

Your choices in the present can overcome *anything* that happened in the past. Know this!

It is the belief that other people and what they did to you are responsible for who you are now, for your emotional pain or your inability to be your true self.

The perpetrators of your past victimized you once. It's up to you whether you remain their victim. They no longer have the power to ruin your life.

The truth is that the only power there is, is contained within this moment: It is the power of your presence.

You have the power to heal. It is an innate capacity you possess as a human being.

Once you know that, you also realize that you are responsible for your inner space now—nobody else is—and that the past cannot prevail against the power of the Now.

Claim your responsibility for your inner space. It's a choice. This book gives you many tools to help you take responsibility for your life.

Please understand this: Only *you* can do this healing. You can get lots of support, but it's up to you. It's your choice. Take that leap of faith to begin the journey.

You are worth it! I believe in you.

MY GRATITUDE

I thank my husband, Paul, for surviving my survival journey with grace, humor and always love. You are the most remarkable person I have ever known and I am blessed to have you in my life. (You are also a great editor!)

To Rusty Duncan Jr., for loving me and giving me a living example of a safe man early in my life. Without you, my childhood would have been far more devastating. You left this earth far too soon. I miss you.

The years spent with Karen Randolph, my therapist, were invaluable. It didn't take four weeks, but it was worth the trip! My deep gratitude for your support of my healing, as well as your feedback on this book.

Linda Weiskoff and Stephanie Ezust have guided hundreds of survivors down the path of healing. I was fortunate enough to be one of them. Thank you for the great gift you give. And, Linda, you still give the best hugs in the world!

Thanks to David Duke, Rusty Duncan Jr., Paul O'Connor, Warren Duncan, and Joe O'Connor for being the kind of men I could put on my original list of five good men in the world. Although the list has expanded considerably, you gave me the faith to open the door. I love you all.

Thanks to Ron Fleisher and Rick Houcek for being number six and seven. And for your enduring friendship.

Most of what I have learned about incest recovery I learned in my incest survivor group. Thanks to all of you special women for sharing your stories. Together we found the path and walked it bravely.

To the Cloud Nine Mastermind—Kevin McDonald, Sonia Stringer, Jim Bunch, Greg Clowmizer, Kevin Lawrence, Andrew Barber-Starkey, and especially Tracy Beckes—for jump-starting this little walk and Teresia LaRocque for saying just the right thing at the right time to keep it moving. All of you have given me the greatest gift—complete acceptance of No-Plan-Nan. Thanks for your love and the safe space you always provide in my life. If I gave birth to this book, then you were the midwives!

My coach, Pam Richarde, believed in this book before it was even a book. Thanks for your love and your faith. And, thanks for the title!

Thanks to my business group, TEC 158, for your support through my life and my writing process. Back when the group was all men, except for Susan and me, you gave me the space and safety to learn to trust men again.

My TEC Associates group was one of the first places I publicly said, "I'm writing a book about incest recovery." Thanks for your warm love and support these last several years.

My life—and those of countless others—would never have attained the heights it has without Thomas Leonard teaching me that all things are possible. Thomas was one of the truly great thinkers of the last century and the world misses his presence.

Shirley Anderson loaned a crucial ear to the initial concepts behind this book. Many thanks for your support and your input into the early draft.

When a professional writer says "You can write," you start to believe. Thanks, Lea Agnew, for reading an early draft and for your penetrating insight. This is a better book because of your generous gift of time and skillful editing.

The Courage to Heal got me through times I wasn't sure I could get through. Many thanks to Ellen Bass and Laura Davis for your groundbreaking work.

My Quaker Friends have helped me understand the stop and go nature of writing this book. They know the value of waiting until the time is right to take the next step. Thank you for your love and support.

Bette Turlington appeared in my life at the perfect moment. Thank you for your love and friendship. I treasure both more than you know.

Special thanks go to my Mother. Thank you for supporting my writing of this book even if it meant telling the family secrets. I appreciate that you are able to support me in that way—many mothers couldn't. I love you.

RECOMMENDED READING

Bass, Ellen and Laura Davis. *The Courage to Heal—Third Edition—Revised and Expanded: A Guide for Women Survivors of Child Sexual Abuse.*

Bradshaw, John. *Homecoming: Reclaiming and Championing Your Inner Child.*

Chodron, Pema. *The Places that Scare You: A Guide to Fearlessness in Difficult Times.*

Chodron, Pema. *When Things Fall Apart: Heart Advice for Difficult Times.*

Chopra, Deepak. *The Seven Spiritual Laws of Success: A Practical Guide to the Fulfillment of Your Dreams.*

Davis, Laura. *The Courage to Heal Workbook: A Guide for Women Survivors of Child Sexual Abuse.*

Gawain, Shakti. *Living in the Light.*

Kabat-Zinn, Jon. *Wherever You Go, There You Are: Mindfulness Meditation in Everyday Life.*

Leonard, Thomas J. *The Portable Coach: 28 Sure Fire Strategies For Business And Personal Success.*

Markova, Dawna. *I Will Not Die an Unlived Life: Reclaiming Purpose and Passion.*

Muller, Wayne. *Legacy of the Heart: The Spiritual Advantage of a Painful Childhood.*

Norwood, Robin. *Women Who Love Too Much.*

Tolle, Eckhart. *The Power of Now: A Guide to Spiritual Enlightenment.*

ABOUT THE AUTHOR

Nan O'Connor walked to the podium amid the cheers of business, media and civic leaders who honored her as a finalist for Entrepreneur of the Year. CEO of one of the country's most respected communication firms, this confident young over-achiever, by all appearances, was on top of the world.

Just an hour before, cheered by a much smaller group, Nan had been on the floor, raging at a large stuffed bear. Long-suppressed anger flowed out. For all the success of her company, this weekly meeting with fellow incest survivors summed up Nan O'Connor's *real* work at the moment—recovering from a childhood of sexual abuse.

Nan now shares her healing journey from devastation to wonderment. Using a format that guides others who must make this frightening yet life-saving journey, Nan tells how she moved from the ravages of hidden memories to the courageous embrace of "incest survivor" as part of who she is. Enhancing the journey, she shares tools and techniques from her current practice as one of America's leading small business coaches.

HELP LEAVE A LEGACY

Long before I knew there was a book for me to write, I had a mission: to do everything in my power to reach out to all those touched by incest and support them in their healing.

Another part of my mission—once I knew I was writing this book—was to get this book into the hands of *every* incest survivor who is seeking to heal.

That's where *you* come in. You can help.

If you found this book useful, please tell others about it. Tell survivors. Tell therapists who work with survivors. Tell support groups. Spread the word that help is at hand.

You can order additional copies of this book at:
www.walkinthewoods.org

And, finally, my mission includes people having the book regardless of their ability to pay. If you would like to buy a book for others, there is a place on the website to do that. We will have a list of people who want a book and can't afford it. When you select the option to buy a book for another survivor, we will send it to the first person on the list. If you wish, we will include your name, so they know from whom it came.

Together, we can do this!

With love,
Nan

Printed in the United States
56532LVS00006B/1-153

9 780977 395002